A CEO's Survival Guide to
Information Technology

A CEO's Survival Guide to
Information Technology

Bob Coppedge

Contents

Acknowledgements

Having never written a book before, I really had no idea what to write here. Acknowledge people for their impact on my life? Or limit to people who impacted this book? Identify people with qualities that I aspire to? Throw in a random stranger or two just to see if people are paying attention?

I'm not sure I've answered this question in my mind. But here goes.

On the professional front, I've had the good fortune to break bread with some of the better minds and souls in the Managed Service Provider (MSP) world. Rob Rae (Datto), Robin Robins (Technology Marketing Toolkit), and Scott Barlow (Sophos), among many others. They may deny knowing me (especially after reading this book), but I know better.

And the world is full of good MSP CEO's. Andrew Sharicz, Bill Whelden, Dave Bell, and Damien Pepper and I meet each week virtually to trade ideas. I mostly provide comic relief (and steal their ideas). Jim Ray is another MSP with some really big ideas and he's the only owner of a redneck BMW that I know of. Be proud, Jim.

I learned a lot (both good and bad) from a couple of bosses, in particular, Bob Schneider and Rick Jones.

Ten years ago, I decided to start a company, Simplex-IT. One of the reasons I was able to pull it off was due to its first employee, Sam Hays, a complete Renaissance Man and one of the sharpest good people I know. When he left Simplex-IT two years later (under good terms), I was extremely concerned, but absolutely lucked out with his replacement, Kevin Dutkiewicz (who is now Tech Director). He and his wife, Sarah Dutkiewicz (who's a Microsoft MVP), are both ridiculously bright and genuinely good people—a really rare combination.

Thanks to all the other people at Simplex-IT who put up with me. Alaa, Cyndee, Doug, Jeff, Kayla, Korrey, Kurt, Michelle, Patti, and Rob, plus all the other folks who have been with Simplex-IT in the past.

And some of the customers who took a chance with us in the early years. Bruce Reibau, Frank Gambosi, and Jim Wagner spring to the forefront.

The three people who shaped me most aren't around to see this book, but I'd like to think they'd be at least a little proud (until they read it, of course):

- My father tried to make me smart
- My mother tried to make me care
- My older sister tried to make me cool

They didn't succeed, but I truly appreciate their efforts.

To all the people I met (and probably annoyed) through the various computer user groups (most notable Greater Cleveland PC Users Group and the Association of PC Users Groups), I say thanks.

From that world, a special thanks to Jim Evans, one of the strongest people I know. On the idolization side of things, thanks to George Carlin and Harlan Ellison. You can care and not be nice. And Richard Burton (the explorer, not the actor), who tried so many things because he could. Specialization is for insects.

And thanks to my younger sister Sarah (who I can still tickle from across a room) and younger brother Paul.

Thanks to all the comedy improvisors both at Second City (Cleveland) and Point of No Return. I never quit my day job.

Finally, in 2003, I had the good fortune, on Independence Day, to switch from single divorced guy to husband, father to three daughters and grandfather (to now five, soon to be six). To daughters Leah, Erin, and Roberta and grandchildren Bryce, Kiley, Hannibal, Matthew, Alex and <to be named later> (as I write this, Roberta is due in two weeks), I say thank you for letting me into your lives.

And finally, leaving the rest in the dust, much love to my wife, Julie. Thanks for keeping me human.

"A CEO's Survival Guide to Information Technology."

1. FOREWORD

Ignorance of technology is the new measure of illiteracy.

Here's the deal. You're a business owner (or you're going to pretend to be while reading this book). You've discovered that it's critical that Information Technology (which, moving forward, we're going to call IT because us geeks love to turn things into its first letter components) is as integrated to your business as effectively as possible, at least to the extent it's not "an afterthought" or "we're forced to use computers." And you've either tried to keep up with technology and ended up spending waaaay too much time (to the point where it's become a "Hobby of the Damned") or you're dependent upon an IT professional that you really, really hope is giving you good advice—and that IT professional might be the guy (or gal) at the office who has a home network (in the land of the blind. . .).

Then you read some articles. You catch stuff from friends and coworkers. You watched an episode of *CSI: Poughkeepsie* (which if it doesn't exist, it should). And somebody mentions a technology gem that you have absolutely no idea about, but it looks like it could either be really cool or really disastrous for your company.

And you really, really hope that your current IT guy (again, or gal) is keeping up—even if that person is you. You find that the resource known as "blind faith" is a well that you keep going to. You hope your IT is as good as it can be. It's secure. It's performing as well as it can and the value you're getting toward your business from IT is as efficient and effective as it should be.

Blind Faith. Do you turn to blind faith in terms of your sales projections? Quality Control? Marketing? Probably not. But IT? It just seems so hard. It seems to be constantly changing. You can't tell if it's getting cheaper or more expensive, and you find that everything and everyone is out to hack everything and everyone else.

That's where I come in. That's where this book comes in.

My name is Bob Coppedge. I'm not a millionaire. I don't have a reality TV show on IT (or business, for that matter). But what I do have is a very particular set of skills, skills I have acquired over a very long career (please imagine me saying that with a really cool Liam Neeson type of voice). I am extremely effective in helping organizations bridge between organizational process and leadership and the village of geeks living on the other side of the organizational moat.

I've been in the IT business since the late 70s, which technically means I'm old. I've worn about every hat, from consultant to IT Director, from Data Base Analyst (DBA) to CIO (Chief Information Officer), programmer and network administrator. Hiring consultants. Being a consultant. Working with end users and in a wide variety of industries, including manufacturing, service, municipal, defense, nonprofits, and healthcare.

The one thing I'm the most capable of is being able to take a look at a process (whether it be technology driven or not) that businesses use and dissect it into its working components, to figure out what works and what doesn't, and why. I'm particularly able to take the geeks' understanding and perspective and communicate it to the business management . . . and vice versa.

My goal is help you, the CEO, understand why the geeks feel what they do in terms of how it impacts your business through three core concepts:

1. **CEO Stuff that Impacts the Geek Side.** What are you using IT for now as it relates to your business? What issues are you dealing with? How do you handle change?
2. **Geek Stuff that Impacts the CEO Side.** You rely on your IT service provider to keep things running. But you have to understand core concepts as it relates to your business. Do they know what *you* consider to be critical in terms of protection or performance?
3. **Now What?** Now that we've opened your eyes, you can look at your organization and IT in a new perspective. Big deal. It's what you do with that knowledge that gives it meaning.

When you engage your IT resources, whether it be a consulting firm, a managed service provider, or your own IT staff (we'll define the difference soon, don't worry), my task is to better arm you with the best way to form questions and how to make sense out of the answers in terms of how it impacts your business. You want to have a strategic understanding between whoever is providing IT services for the organization, and those depending on those services, *starting with you.* You need a strategic perspective on technology, which *doesn't include deep tech knowledge.* I'm going to begin helping you build that foundation, without just relying on someone else. That's not delegation; that's abdication. And you can't do that, not in todays' changing tech environment.

No Tech Teaching Here

Are you going to learn the real tech stuff here? Ahhh . . . no. First of all, that means this book is out of date before it's even finished. What we *are* going to talk about is the high-altitude concepts of the technology. What are the core components, and how do they directly relate to critical aspects of your business? Why the time to recover data is important, not the technology behind providing it. You'll still need to rely on technology professionals to provide your solutions, but you'll know *what your solutions need to accomplish and why.*

And we're going to focus on small-medium businesses, or SMBs. Why? Well, honestly, because the big guys have the bucks and resources (and requirements) to deal with these big IT issues with correspondingly big $ budgets, unlike the smaller blokes like us. But the issues are just as critical.

Most books I've seen on IT topics are either written with the goal of explaining the technology (so they're obsolete before they're done) or from such a conceptual standpoint that they don't represent a real-world perspective.

I've seen many organizations where all the IT pieces are working "properly." Servers are chugging away, printers are printing gobs of data and a ton of money is spent on all sorts of boxes with fancy lights, loud fans, and the continuous need for patching, upgrading and "turning it on and turning it back on again." But they don't seem to truly add value to the organization in a direct manner (indirect is pretty much good enough rounding up, doncha think?). Any asked individual (whether technologist or business folk) will say something either dismissive ("it wasn't built for that") or wistful ("yeah, it would be cool if it was built for that").

The big corporations can afford to pay big bucks for a lot of these concepts. There's tons of stuff out there for the true corporate world: millions of dollars in the budget and strategic plans out the tuchus. And let's face it. Your 5-year plan is probably light on the IT side, with goals stated like "upgrade server" or "redesign website." I've spoken to a couple hundred business owners and executives over the past 30 years or so who had this type of conversation, and there have been a number of them who have actually taught me a thing or two about how IT impacts organizations in ways that I never considered.

Why Did I Write This?

I wrote *A CEO's Survival Guide to Information Technology* out of the frustration I'd experience when talking about the challenges and problems that business owners have with their IT. We IT folks have a reputation of being condescendingly arrogant, overbearing, and aloof with understanding the full atmosphere of the business, and an aspect of that it is absolutely deserved. If you disagree, you must be stupid (that felt good!). We're much more concerned with being accurate than being understood. But you CEO's don't get off scot free, either! Part of it is also because CEOs don't feel they *need* (or in many cases *want*) to take the time to understand. These are conversations I've had over and over again (sometimes with the same CEO, oddly enough). I've never known of anybody who actually wrote from the perspective of the CEO trying to manage their IT problems, except to teach the CEO about IT.

The best example of the CEO/IT relationship comes in the form of this story. A CEO went to a county fair and decided to take a balloon ride, but there was a bit of a snafu. He got in the balloon just as the rope up and snapped. The balloon took off by itself. Now the CEO's freaking out about how to deal with the balloon. But then he relaxes and floats over the park for a bit, no problem. Meanwhile, he sees a bystander who happened to be walking down a path in the park. The CEO yells down, "Hey, down there! Can you help me?"

The guy down below yells up, "Yeah, I can help you. You're up in a balloon. You're floating around aimlessly and you can't get down." The business owner says, "Shit. You must be an IT guy . . ." The guy said, "Yeah . . . and how do you know that?" The business owner replies, "Because everything you told me is absolutely accurate, 100 percent spot on, and completely no use to me whatsoever." And the guy replies, "Well, yeah you must be a business owner. And you know how I know that? Because you're the guy stuck up there in the balloon, you've got no way down, and somehow it's *my* fault."

Feel like taking a balloon ride with me? C'mon . . . you know you want to.

2. INTRODUCTION

This is a survival guide to the business world of information technology. Although it's intended for the CEO of a small-to-medium business, anyone with interest in this topic should benefit (especially me if you bought this book—which, of course, you should. Several copies, in fact).

Okay, anecdotal time. First of all, you should know that all of the stories in this book are inspired by real events that I experienced. I'm tweaking some of the details (like names), but the gist is real.

Being a small business owner in today's world of entrepreneurship is as rewarding as it is terrifying—the biggest challenge being that you *have* to change. Everything is changing, no matter what you're doing in business today. Change rules the day. Change rules our existence, *especially* the IT reality. In some ways, it's much easier for small businesses to change and to adapt, to work in new things than it is for larger businesses. That's the good news. The bad news is that if you're not prepared, change can overwhelm you. So the opportunities for those who can embrace change and take advantage of it are absolutely tremendous. There will also be failures. There will be frustrations. There will be risks. There will be losses.

And that's okay.

The way we used to do things doesn't work anymore. In IT, this is like talking to somebody pre-industrial revolution versus post-industrial revolution. An organization based on muscle was overwhelmed by a competitor who used James Watts' steam engine. It's similar to what's going on today, but the speed of change today is overwhelmingly faster. Imagine a teen today talking to a telephone operator about their job (ask your parents). With the industrial revolution, the change, however profound, took a generation (or two, depending on how you measured) to really take hold. And the business value of muscle took a huge hit.[1]

Now we're having the same situation, except the brain and paper has been replaced with systems powered by technology. And the flexibility of the process both from a development and delivery standpoint (relative to "the dark ages" . . . like the 80's) makes the delivery of new ideas, new goods and services, and new entire concepts extremely dynamic.

And you ain't seen nothin' yet.

---

[1] For a great description between today's Information Revolution and the Industrial Revolution, I highly recommend "The Second Machine Age: Work, Progress, and Prosperity in a Time of Brilliant Technologies" by Erik Brynjolfsson and Andrew McAfee

3. WHY IS IT IMPORTANT?

The Best/Worst of Times. . .

This is part of why it's so fantastic to be a small business today. If you take a look at any part of the real picture, we are becoming more and more a service economy. Even if we are producing goods, our goods are still provided as part of the service. And there's actually a third component that's being added . . . the customer *experience* while gaining the goods and services. But more on that later.

Oh, and that's why it also sucks to be a small business today. If you don't have at least a passing understanding of information technologies in terms of impact on your goods and services and delivery thereof, well . . . your competition will. And soon.

Why is that? I hope I don't have to explain the amount of change that's gone through the IT world over the past couple of decades. Every aspect of sharing data and information (we'll talk about the difference soon) has increased in terms of flexibility, accessibility, and accuracy, while decreased in terms of cost, skillset needed to consume, and applicability. So today small 1-3 employee organizations are using business intelligence tools for $20/month that only a decade ago Fortune 500 companies were implementing with a multi-million dollar budget.

The quantity and quality of tools available to the average small business are staggering. And you ain't seen nothing yet.

Progress

Here's the thing. These changes have happened not only during my lifetime, but during the lifetime of my career. So change, significant, mind-bending, "time to rewrite the book" change is, well . . . unchanging.

But not consistently. Companies adopt new concepts at different rates, based on geography, vertical market need, age, even health of an organization. In 2016, we were talking with manufacturing companies that were only then looking to replace servers that were running with software produced in the 90's. And they were still profitable! Because the technology worked for their product and mission, they saw no reason to invest in upgrading.

And that's . . . okay-ish. If the company is appropriately profitable to the owners, provides a compelling good and/or service combination to the customer, and reasonably satisfies the needs of all other stakeholders, who are we to argue? The "-ish" is added because . . . well, it's there because of the looming question: "*Why* haven't you upgraded?" Often it ain't the action, it's the reasoning behind the action that's more telling.

It could be that upgrading the technology would significantly increase the positive aspects of the company (profitability, safety, size, market longevity).

IT makes it exceedingly easier for companies to scale, measure, and report on efforts and processes—but only if it is working hand in hand with your actual process.

4.   YOUR IT PARTNER

As I stated earlier, I'm not going to try to teach you all the nuances and technologies represented in IT. First of all, that's not your goal. Second, there are a ton of books that already do that. Finally, IT changes. Daily. So I'd be out of date before I published.

When you need legal advice (and you're not a lawyer), do you just Google it? Or accounting advice or tax advice? No (or at least I hope not). And keep in mind that the rate of change (and increase in complexity) in law and tax pale in comparison to the rate of change for IT. So depending on how dependent we are on the particular skill, we develop a relationship with a resource that has that skill.

You need to develop that type of relationship for your IT needs. I'm not talking about just someone to fix stuff that is broken. That's like hiring a handyman plumber to design and install the entire plumbing for a water park. The handyman is great for fixing stuff. But not in determining the best and most efficient water flow for a super slide.

You want someone who will understand your business, what your business needs and goals are, and can then relate them to the appropriate IT tools that are out-and available.

But I've Got this Book?

What I'm trying to do here is help you ask better questions of your IT resource. And make sure that you're making the decisions that you should be making, and your IT resource is making the decisions they should be making.

So here are some options for your IT Resource (more details on these options later).

a. **You and Google.** C'mon. Get serious. Every minute you spend on your IT is a minute you're not spending on developing your business. And trust me, you're not as good at this as you think you are.

b. **Vendors.** Organizations that you bring on to do specific tasks or install particular equipment/systems/services. The challenge with them is that their goal is to do a job, finish it up, get paid and move on.

c. **Internal IT Staff.** Employee(s). For smaller organizations, this often means only one person. The challenge then is that they are spread so thin that they spend all their time keeping things running. Skill sets are often just "good enough" to keep things running. Future projects (or business expansion) isn't in their sights (unless you make that a priority).

d. **Managed Services.** An agreement delegating the internal IT responsibilities to a third party (usually called the MSP or Managed Service Provider) for a fixed monthly fee. Usually, this approach strongly favors a sweeping proactive approach to IT management. Unfortunately, the definition is becoming more inconsistent by the day. Properly implemented, it's a popular choice for many businesses.

e. **Co-Managed IT Services.** One of the newest buzzwords, I find this one pretty interesting. A combination of Managed Services and Internal IT Staff. It's a way (when properly implemented) to get the best of both worlds.

Let's Compare the Resources

Okay, I'm going to be honest here. As the owner of a Managed Services firm (Simplex-IT), I'm a little biased over both the value and definition of Managed Services.

Here's our scenario. You're driving down a street, and right in the middle of the road, something fretful is in the way—a board with a big nail sticking out of it, which you run over, puncture a tire, swerve out of control, and smack right into a telephone pole.

If it's **You and Google**, um . . . good luck with that. Hope you've got a good signal wherever you crashed.

Then you've got the traditional "this got broken, now let's fix it" logic with the **Vendor** solution. The accident happens, so you look up a number for a local garage; hopefully, they're still open. You arrange for a tow truck and probably a rental car. The costs add up, but a solution has been reached. It eventually gets fixed, and the driver gets back on the road.

If this accident hadn't happened, you would be out $0. But since it did happen, you lost that time, which is the most valuable of all assets. Which brings us back to the old universal maxim: time is money. In my opinion, that thought has actually reversed. Now, it's *money is time*. You're out the time your car was out of commission, plus the tow truck costs. Plus, any additional damage costs. That's the traditional ideology: we're waiting for something to break and then we'll fix it.

If you have an **Internal IT staff**, it depends on the size and skill set of your staff. Do they have the time to fix the car immediately? Do they have the skill set necessary? You're still out the down time and expenses.

A **Managed Services** arrangement is a preventative solution (when properly implemented). There's no nail sticking out of a board for you to run over. Someone has taken responsibility, and this is where that engagement occurs. The Managed Service Provider (MSP) has taken responsibility for the organization and makes sure that there are no hazards in the way. Some people conclude that since nothing happened, an MSP agreement is a waste of money! The truth is that this preventative maintenance with this preventative mentality prevented the downtime and any cost from damages. That's the strategy that's both most effective and efficient. And we want to get away from the mentality of just hiring somebody to fix it because again money is time. We want to be as productive as possible. It's the use of our time that is increasing the productivity, not the money.

A Managed Services Agreement creates a relationship between your organization and the MSP (Managed Services Provider). That relationship defines responsibility in terms of service and expectations in return for a monthly fee. Most MSP's have an extensive team that have a lot more experience (and specific expertise) than most SMB's will have with their own IT employees. And the agreement should include the responsibility that the MSP will understand your business goals, goods, and services.

The **Co-Managed IT Services** (CoMITs) is where an organization has both Internal IT Employees and an MSP agreement, cooperating as a team. We've been successfully applying this strategy for years, and it currently accounts for about 20% of our customers. I think this model will be common in the next 5-10 years.

Summary:

- There are several strategies that companies use for IT support. Identify yours. Is it working for you?
- Is the relationship you have with your IT partner a successful one? Could it be better?

5. DEFINITIONS

Before we get started, it might help to bring some definition to terms we'll be revisiting. Entire books have been written about each of these concepts, and the definitions I'm using could be challenged on many levels. But I think they'll work for the purposes of this book.

Complexity

One of the concepts I like to bring up when discussing IT processes is "complexity." The Oxford Dictionary defines complexity as "the state or quality of being intricate or complicated *as it pertains to a business process or product.*" Okay, I added the italicized words for purposes of this book. Let's add some meat to it:

1. Complexity adds cost (measured in increased time, money) to the process or product.
2. Added Complexity without added value is detrimental to an organization.
3. Complexity can be simply measured by the concept of "how many words do you need to accurately describe it?"
4. Creeping Complexity plagues many organizations. Steps, processes, and exceptions that have been added over the years for those rare special (and often unprofitable) cases.

One of the big points here is #3. Notice that I'm keeping the definition of Complexity simple. It's actually a pretty helpful mind exercise. Let's look at two examples of "How do you find your year-to-date sales?"

Goofus: *"Easy-Peasy. First, our Sales Manager has to run our sales reports for the year, then creates an Excel worksheet. She then* edits them in case we have any prior year adjustments (because they show up as negative sales in our ytd reports). Then the Office Manager enters the info from the worksheet into QuickBooks. Our Accountant then matches that against the banking info and blesses the numbers. Then I run the sales report."

Gallant: "Every night, we have a set of automated processes that integrate the information between systems. So every day I've got accurate figures from the night before."

We don't need to do a word count to see that Goofus (we'll see more of these two blokes later on) has the more complex process to answer the same question.

By the way, I know that having a single system that integrates everything (i.e., an ERP or Enterprise Resource Planning, system) would solve these issues, but where's the fun in that here? Seriously, we'll discuss plusses and minuses of fully integrated systems later on.

IT processes that run hand in hand with the Business processes of an organization maintain, control, and minimize the negative aspects of complexity. If IT and Business are at odds with each other, the complexity is increased without adding value.

Data

He was an android who wanted . . . never mind. Data is one of those terms that is thrown around loosely (like "cloud" or "server") and hard to pin down. For the purposes of this book, there are really two types of data.

1. **Application Data.** In most cases, when a company is running an application that creates value for the company and stakeholders (i.e., customers and vendors),

some record of the activity is recorded in the form of application data. Accounting, inventory, and payroll applications are all examples, creating a good amount of data stored in their systems. We then can use tools to aggregate, filter, and present data to create useful information (and make decisions, often automatically).

2. **Freeform Data.** This is data in the form of documents— Word processing documents, spreadsheets, presentations, CAD drawings. These are usually created using applications, but these applications are more controlled by the single user. Freeform data originally was difficult to "mine" in terms of reporting, but tools are getting better and better at doing just that.

Data Versus Information

This is my own definition and a tool I use when discussing the difference between gathering data and using information. As a former (and failed, I might add) Physics Major, data is "Potential Energy" and Information is "Kinetic Energy."

Data is a collection of values gathered through traditional business processes and operations. It's sitting there, not doing anything—data concerning customers, vendors, orders, products. It becomes "Information" when it's used, bringing additional value to the organization.

Example:

The Cleveland Heights, Ohio White Pages telephone book (ask your parents) contains data (name, address, phone #) about all residents within the city of Cleveland Heights, Ohio. The Information would be a specific entry pulled out as a query by someone wanting to order a pizza.

We create, gather, and use Data. We use Information.

Goods and Services

As any Business 101 course or book will tell you, the term "goods and services" is a loose definition of what an organization or individual provides that creates a value for their customers. Okay, that's pretty straightforward. The only point I would make here is it's almost *never* only "goods," but it *can* be only "services." The day that an organization only creates products (i.e., manufacturing) without some level of accompanying value-adding services is pretty much gone. The services might be wrapped around pre-order customization or extreme flexibility in delivering, but the services are becoming more and more the flagbearer of the question, "What is the unique value proposition for your organization?"

IT

First of all, anybody who believes they fully understand IT most certainly does not. Physicist Richard Feynman said about quantum mechanics, *"If you think you understand quantum mechanics, you don't understand quantum mechanics."* The same is true here. IT is so dynamic and so changing that it's simply impossible to keep up with all trends in all industries dealing with IT.

You don't *have* to understand either. I want to help you become comfortable in *not* knowing. You just need to grasp some of the core concepts as a whole, so when you talk to a technologist whose job it is to understand the core concepts of the technology of that particular subtype of IT that you're looking at, they can explain things and you absorb enough to have a framework of functional thinking to manage your overarching role as CEO, and understand enough concepts to appreciate how it's going to prove itself to you.

But again, what is IT, anyway? If we headed back to Oxford, they'd say: "Information technology (IT) is the application of computers to store, retrieve, transmit, and manipulate data, often in the context of a business or other enterprise."

I'd say the definition is about 10-20 years out of date. We'll get into specifics on what I mean by that later on, but for now this'll do. If we're presenting/manipulating/transmitting data using computers (including tablets, phones, laptops, desktops, Internet-enabled devices), it's fair game.

Information Technology is really the use of technology to help us measure and assist in the creation and production of the goods and the services. The technology allows us to deal with ever increasingly complicated matters. And it does so in such a way that we can use the data that's generated from these processes and really answer some dynamic questions about business.

All that aside, we'll be breaking down IT into some bite-sized components in a bit. Hang in there.

Stakeholders

Notice I didn't say "customers" or "employees" or "vendors" (nor did I say "ostriches," though the temptation was palpable). Stakeholders is a broader definition in that it includes all parties that are directly impacted by the success (or failure) of an organization or project. Far too often, I've seen companies become way too focused on one group of stakeholders, to the detriment of the rest. The only way an organization can thrive and succeed long-term is through a balanced approach. But who are the stakeholders? My simple list would include:

- **Customers.** People and organizations that partake in the good and services that the organization provides.
- **Vendors.** People and organizations that provide good and services that the organization consumes.
- **Employees.** People who provide regular services for the organization in return for wages or salary.
- **Management.** Employees with an organization in a position of control, responsibility, and decision-making, especially for long-term direction.
- **Owners.** People and organizations that own the organization.
- **Public.** The remainder of society, which could be potential Customers, Vendors and Employees.

Information Technology impacts (as we'll see) how an organization connects and relates with each of these categories.

Value

Ahhh, that brings up value, another concept that I like to try to define. How can we talk about adding value to an organization through IT without defining what the heck value is, anyway?

Once again, I like to keep it simple. My definition of value is measured by:

1. Increasing Revenue
2. Decreasing Costs
3. Maintaining/Improving Infrastructure

Now, I'm not going to spend a lot of time defending what revenue, costs, or infrastructure are, because that's really dependent on the organization. A non-profit helping the unfortunate might define revenue as providing their services, instead of improving inbound cash. And that's absolutely cool.

So when we talk about "adding value" through implementation of IT, the above list is how we're going to define it.

Summary:

- Many of the terms above have multiple definitions, depending on the perspective and context.

6. IT DEVICES AND COMMON TERMS

This section is similar to the previous, but I'm going to try to define the various pieces and parts of devices (physical or otherwise) and services that you probably already have within your organization.

a. **BioMetrics**. Biometrics (in this context) is the use of biological traits to identify a user. Fingerprint, voice, and facial recognition are the three most common traits used today.

b. **Cloud.** As is often the case, we (the industry) have taken a technology term and hyped it up beyond recognition. "The Cloud" has been in existence for as long as the Internet. When you visit the website of an organizations, the website is located in "the cloud." Although it can be argued, for purposes of this book, "The Cloud" is a collection of IT resources that are offered, stored, and managed by third parties on their own managed equipment. The alternative to Cloud is On Premise.

c. **Desktop.** A (usually) non-portable computing device accessed by end users. It transcends manufacturers, so computers manufactured by Apple, Dell, HP or hobbled together as a hobby are considered desktops.

d. **Device.** For these discussions, a device is any kind of . . . um . . . device that sends or receives electronic data through a network, including the Internet.

e. **Encryption.** A method used to protect data, whether at rest (stored on a disk) or en route (an email sent to another party) from inappropriate access.

f. **EndPoint Protection.** A term used to describe security software loaded on end user devices. Anti-virus software is a form of EndPoint protection.

g. **Exploit.** An exploit (usually a technique used in a malware application) takes advantage of a vulnerability to access or infect a computer or component. When that vulnerability is fixed (through a patch or better configuration), that exploit becomes ineffective. As an example, if you build a 15-foot wall, a 16-foot ladder would be an exploit.

h. **File Synchronization.** A popular service for both consumer and business. Synchronization automatically takes file changes made on one device and copies (um, synchronizes) the changes to one or multiple other sites. DropBox is an example of a consumer-based file synchronization service (although they've added some corporate level functionality of late). This has three primary benefits:

　　a. Allows users to have access to their files on multiple devices

　　b. Users can securely share files between themselves and others

　　c. Serves as a backup in case the original device is lost or destroyed

i. **Firewall.** This device is a layer of protection used to control data flowing between networks (or between your organization and the Internet). Firewalls (and their successors, "Unified Threat Management" (UTM) devices) have increased significantly in power and complexity over recent years in response to increased cyber attacks.

j. **FTP.** File Transfer Protocol. This technique, although outdated, is still used by many organizations to transfer files between organizations. It has significant security limitations and has been replaced by multiple more flexible and secure options.

k. **Hub.** A device used to transfer data between multiple devices with little or no management or monitoring capabilities. A USB hub allows several USB devices to connect to a single USB port on a computer. A networking hub allows several devices to be connected to a network. A networking hub is much less expensive than a switch, but is commonly the creator of networking performance issues and should be avoided.

l. **ISP.** Internet Service Provider. These organizations provide services that connect your organization to the Internet. Several methods are used (i.e., DSL, T1, fiber, cable). High speed options are opening up daily, and competition is fierce.

m. **Key.** A key is a unique value that's provided for various purposes. For encryption, it's used to decrypt devices and emails. For licensing, it's to validate a software purchase. Make sure you keep track of your licensing keys.

n. **Laptop.** A portable desktop, usually with an attached keyboard. Laptops are usually identical to a desktop in terms of software.

o. **Linux.** Linux is a software product used to run servers. Most servers are running either a version of Linux of Microsoft Windows Server.

   • **Malware.** Malware is software designed to be malevolent. Ten years ago or so, our primary definition of

Malware was "virus," and we used the terms interchangeably. Nowadays, viruses are a category of Malware (since the bad guys have gotten significantly more creative). Back in the day, the goal of Malware was as a prank or sabotage. Nowadays, it's taken a more commercial bent, with the goal to make money (a lot more on that later). Malware is often defined in the following categories[2], which define their method, not their goal:

- ○ **Trojan Horses.** Evil software "hides" in seemingly legitimate software.
- ○ **Viruses.** Evil software usually attached to a file that will replicate itself to other computers, "infecting them."
- ○ **Worms.** Self-replicating evil software, but not requiring a separate piece of software, like Trojans or Viruses.
- ○ **Bots.** A bot is an application that is installed on an infected device that runs automated tasks at the bidding of a "bot master." A workstation infected with a bot is often referred to as a "zombie."

p. **Managed Device.** A managed device is a device on a network that is not dedicated to a user function, nor a server. It's considered a "managed" device if it has the capability to report performance metrics or alerts to specific software created to manage the devices remotely. The goal for all but the smallest networks is to have all devices be managed devices.

q. **Mobile Device.** A mobile phone.

---

[2] From Sophos's Threatsaurus: https://www.sophos.com/en-us/security-news-trends/security-trends/threatsaurus.aspx

r. **Multi-Factor Authentication (or Two-Factor Authentication).** For years, we've depended on the good old account name and password to get you into systems. No more. In order to combat cyber threats, many organizations are requiring multiple factors to get in. As an example, you may need to know a password *and* swipe your fingerprint (that would make it two factors). Or the system will text your phone a special key when you use your password and swipe your fingerprint (now we're up to three).

s. **Network.** A network usually indicates a bunch of devices that can be configured to communicate with each other without too much difficulty and complexity. So all of the devices within your primary locations make up a "network." The term could be only talking about your wireless devices (your "wireless network"). Networks can be divided or combined, depending on the need.

t. **On Premise.** Also known as "On Prem," this is where the equipment is on site. This has been the default location for a majority of IT resources until "The Cloud" introduced compelling reasons to migrate equipment and services off site. On Prem is usually owned by the organization, but not always (see "blank as a Service" in Section 3).

u. **OS (Operating System).** This is the primary set of software that's running on your desktop, laptop, tablet, mobile device, or server. Without it, nothing works. Windows 10, Windows Server, Linux, iPhone, and MacOS are some examples.

v. **Patching.** No software is released without problems or "bugs." Software vendors release fixes to the bugs in the form of "patches," which are (usually) downloaded and applied. Some vendors do this automatically, some leave it up to the end user (or the internal IT resource). Patches are also frequently introduced to plug up security leaks discovered after the software was released, as well as new features.

w. **RAID.** Redundant Array of Independent Disks[3]. This is a technique of using multiple hard drives (where we store data on workstations and servers) to both boost performance (two heads are faster than one) and protect against failure. An example is a Mirrored array (Raid 1). This is when you are writing to two identical drives simultaneously. If one fails, the other continues to work while you replace the drive. Very popular (I'd say a necessity) with servers.

x. **Router.** This device takes data transmitted from a device and "routes" it to another network. Often Routers and Firewalls are combined into a single device now called a UTM.

y. **SSD.** This stands for Solid State Drive, a hard drive storage device with no moving parts. Data is stored electronically. Traditional hard drives have spinning disks and moving heads that read data off the drives. SSD's are significantly faster, but with much smaller storage space.

z. **Switch.** The traffic cop for data traffic. This is the device that has all the data cables plugged into it. A switch has ports (usually 16, 24, or 48), each of which can connect a device on the other end to all other devices connected to the switch. Switches can be combined or "stacked" so

---

[3] For more info see https://en.wikipedia.org/wiki/RAID

that hundreds of devices can be connected inside your organization. Switches are both Managed and Unmanaged, with Managed being much preferable (and a bit more expensive).

aa. **Tablet.** A tablet is a smaller laptop, often without an actual keyboard. And many tablets are running on lower power hardware than a laptop, meaning that they can't run the same types of applications or have the same storage or processing power. These tablets are usually either Android or iPad based. There are tablets that are fully-functional Windows 10-based tablets, although these are either more expensive or really low-powered.

bb. **Unmanaged Devices.** An unmanaged device is a device on a network that is not dedicated to a user function, nor a server. Unlike a managed device, these don't have the capability to report performance metrics or alerts to specific software created to manage the devices remotely. They just do what they can, and if they run into problems, they tell or alert nobody. Yeah, they're cheap. But stay away from them if you can (especially for switches).

cc. **VOIP.** Voice Over Internet Protocol. Older phones transmitted the voices on a phone call by converting the sound waves to electrical current over copper wires as an analog signal. Worked great, but didn't scale well. VOIP converts the voice into data packets containing bits (0's and 1's), sends them along IT networks like any other data (mostly), and then converts the transmitted data back to voice on the receiving end.

dd. **VPN.** Virtual Private Networks. If you have devices on different networks communicating through the Internet, their communications can be (relatively) easily listened in on. A VPN creates a virtual tunnel between the two locations where all data is securely encrypted. This allows users to access network resources on the road and organizations with multiple locations to share resources between them. Keep in mind that VPN's do nothing to help with performance.

ee. **WAP (Wireless Access Point).** This device is used to connect devices to your network wirelessly. WAPs have grown up significantly over the years, providing additional layers of security (so guests can only go out to the Internet, while employees can access servers and printers). They have a limited range (based on a number of factors). Most decent WAP devices can be combined. This means that a user who connected their wireless device to a WAP can move through your office and be serviced by another WAP device that they stray near.

ff. **Workstation.** Another term for desktop. Some people use the term workstation to refer to more powerful desktops (for CAD or graphic design applications).

Summary:

- A majority of these terms you don't need on a daily basis (if at all). Some of them will come up throughout the book, or when dealing with your IT partner.

- As before, some of these definitions for these terms are subject to perspective. Your mileage may vary.

PART I

CEO Stuff that Impacts the Geek Side

Introduction:

CEOs are the top dog. They're the ones who, at the end of the day, are responsible for making sure (directly or indirectly) that the trains are running, and that the trains are going where they are supposed to be, with timeliness and accuracy toward their destination. And they're carrying what they're supposed to be carrying. This is especially true for the small-to-medium CEO. I'm not saying they have to be *the* expert on all aspects within the organization. The opposite is true, especially if the organization plans to grow. But the CEO has to have *some* knowledge on all aspects of the organization. And the more critical the process, the more the CEO should have some level of understanding.

The problem is that in a number of cases the CEO is blindly dependent upon Information Technology for providing their service resources appropriately. There is often a lack of focused preparation, planning and understanding. This all affects how those services are delivered. It would be kind of like you would never see a CEO who's dependent upon sales say, "Okay, guys, go out and sell stuff. Let me know when it's sold." And then let it go for six to twelve months. Yet, you have that kind of abdication that happens frequently because the CEO doesn't understand IT.

"Aw, crap," I hear you cry. "I have to become a geek?!" Ah . . . no. That's overkill. But you have to understand which critical IT decisions are business-leaning in nature versus IT-leaning. You need to understand IT well enough from a conceptual standpoint. Leave the details to us geeks.

Similarly, you need to keep *us* from doing *your* job. A lot of geeks think they know the business needs from an IT perspective as well as you (especially if you aren't helping any). We end up with a blind guy describing the landscape while the deaf guy listens.

The CEO needs to have a basic knowledge of all operations, and I'm talking about basic knowledge—not huge, Einstein level understanding. Especially if you look at organizations and if you simply ask the what-if question: as in, what if this resource disappeared for a period of time . . . would your company be freaking out?

The answer almost universally is, "Absolutely, we'd be at a freaking standstill!" If you have that level of vulnerability, then you bloody well better understand some aspects about how that works and where your vulnerability is. Look at other factors, as well. If your organization is going to be looking for a 15 percent annual growth in revenue, and that growth is going to be achieved by the diversification of the product line, at the same time we're going to be engaging salespeople on the outside *and* we're going to be beefing up the social media. All of these things are dependent upon Information Technology expanding and supporting those needs and requirements.

If the CEO does not understand—and again I'm talking about the core concepts with the core requirements behind them—how can they be engaged in the decision making in terms of what the prioritization should be?

In this section, we're going to go over some common issues from the CEO's perspective:

1. What does *your* current IT look like?
2. What's the impact of IT in your business?
3. What *should* IT mean in your business?
4. IT is not your Business. Your Information Technology processes don't match up with your Business processes.
5. IT and Obsolescence.
6. Henry Ford's Nightmare. You can have any car you want, as long as it's black. NOT.
7. CEO Whining Points. Common themes I hear from CEO's dealing with IT issues.

Think I'm being hard on management? Talking down, being condescending? *Well* . . . maybe a little (for purposes of this book only, of course). But the fact is, they're often idiots when it comes to IT.

And that's understandable. We're all idiots. Welcome to the club. I've often referred to life as a "Circle of Idiots." All of us are woefully unprepared for many topics, realities, and situations. I have no idea how to repair a car, use power tools, change a diaper (I outsourced my kids), do taxes, work with health insurance, plan a party, dance, rap (I've tried . . . not pretty), work at a fast food place (seriously, I respect folks who can), cook, repair anything, or tie a bow tie. On each of those topics, I'm a complete and total idiot. Guilty as charged.

But I'll never pretend to be otherwise. I have embraced my inner idiot. I know enough to ask my tax preparer quasi-intelligent questions. I have a wife that's a wiz at power tools (and with kids, although separate skill sets to be sure).

Summary:

- You don't need to be a geek. You don't need to be an expert. But you need to have enough information about the topic so that you, as CEO, can weigh your priorities against your options when dealing with IT challenges and opportunities.

7. WHAT IS IT?

In the past chapter, I gave a general definition of Information Technology. Great. But let's face it, I gave a pretty vague definition. I mean, it's not hard to understand Information Technology from a gut level. But is there a better way we can define IT by categorizing the purpose of the IT components being used in your organization?

Note: You can skip this section if you want to stay away from the geek stuff as much as possible. But this isn't going that deep into the geek. I promise.

I had the opportunity on Nov 9, 2017, to hear a keynote address by Arnie Bellini, ConnectWise CEO, at the 2017 IT Nation conference[4]. ConnectWise is one of the major vendors in the Managed Service Provider world, and Arnie is recognized as one of the main voices (and visionaries, a description I don't often use). He spoke to the 3,500 or so (including yours truly) on the state of the industry.

He did a great job of taking the vast array of devices, applications, services, buzzwords, strategies, and approaches aimed at business that are constantly in a state of change. He broke IT down into 14 components in terms of purpose, referring to it as the "technology canvas" for business. They are illustrated in the graphic below (recreated from Arnie's keynote):

---

[4] Wanna watch the keynote?: https://youtu.be/QFMzNAL69Y4. The second half is mostly about products for MSP's, but the first half is useful to everybody trying to compartmentalize IT for the purpose of this topic.

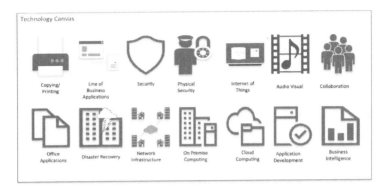

Not all companies use all 14, and any IT product might (and often will) fit under several components. Microsoft's Office 365, for example, has its toes in Collaboration, Office Applications, Onsite Computing, Cloud Computing, and Business Intelligence. I think it's important for CEO's to have at least a modest understanding of these components of IT. So here goes (the specific definitions, by the way, are mine):

Copy/Printing. Yup, we're talking Guttenberg here. Despite the repeated calls for "paperless office," the computer continues to be no friend to trees.

Line of Business Applications. These are software applications (usually purchased or rented from third parties) that are critical to an organization's ability to provide goods and services to their customers.

Security. This component protects the data and information created, modified, shared and consumed from observation, theft, manipulation, or destruction by inappropriate third parties.

Physical Security. This is security equipment communicating through IT networks. We're talking security cameras, audio sensors, and similar devices.

Internet of Things. These are devices (and their services) that provide data without human intervention. Smart refrigerators, cars, drones, and shop floor devices are all providing data (and possible security challenges).

Audio/Visual. The technology that creates much of the marketing and entertainment presentation has made leaps and bounds.

Collaboration. Working together (whether two people or many people), regardless of location, has become a critical need for organizations trying to seamlessly take advantage of skills and resources across the globe. And Arnie included (and I agree with him) all things phones here, including mobile and VOIP.

Disaster Recovery. The precautions necessary (not just in technology, but throughout the organization) to minimize the interruption and damage caused by any unplanned outage of services or destruction of data. I prefer the term "Business Continuity," but I'm going to stick with Arnie on his definitions here.

Office Applications. These are the traditional applications that create value within an organization. The flagship for this is Microsoft Office (word processing, spreadsheets, presentation, email), although Google's toolset provides much of the same functionality (as do other offerings from smaller companies).

Network Infrastructure. This is the collection of devices and services that keep the data flowing effectively and securely. Switches, routers, firewalls, wireless access points, cabling. This stuff isn't sexy, but absolutely critical in terms of performance and security.

Onsite Computing. Computing resources located internally or "On Premise" for the organization. For the foreseeable future, connecting to devices located at the same location will be easier to secure and faster than connecting between different locations. This would be the "On Prem" servers and workstations.

Cloud Computing. This would be computing resources located externally or "Off Premise" for the organization. For organizations where multiple locations want to connect to their resources (an organization with a large remote salesforce or a site selling to the public at large), Cloud Computing presents several benefits.

Application Development. Notice the word "Development." We're talking about resources that are being used to write the code and create applications for users (whether within the organization or beyond) to run.

Business Intelligence. There are many tools that are available (many at little or no cost) for small-to-medium businesses to read data from their applications, vendors, or third parties, and then transpose that data into meaningful and insightful information about your organization.

Now Arnie's audience was a roomful of technology consultants—his customers. The goal was to categorize the IT solutions that MSP's can offer, giving MSP's the ability to focus on what they're best at delivering.

But I think this model of IT presents another opportunity, and that is to categorize the stack of IT services in a way that non-IT management can better understand the wide array of IT products, goods, and services that impact the organization.

Let's be clear. It's not important to have an exact understanding of each of these. That's where your IT resources come in. But it is critical, as a CEO, for you to have a general conception of the category and how it impacts your organization. And then we'll give bonus points for seeing where there's opportunity to be gained by increasing your use of a specific category.

One note on Onsite and Cloud Computing. It's not an "either/or" solution. Most companies are finding that the hybrid model (some Cloud, some Onsite) works best for their organizational needs.

Keep in mind, this wasn't necessarily Arnie's goal of creating his list. But it struck me that this categorization tool[5] would be a great way for a non-technical CEO (that would be you, gentle reader) to approach IT from a 30,000-foot view.

Here's a quick quiz. Take Bob's IT Self-Assessment quiz. Three steps. Use a grading scale of 1-5 (5 being most positive, 1 being most negative), "n/a" (not applicable) or "d/k" (don't know). For each of these categories:

1. **How critical is this category to your organization?** For example, not all organizations are using IT for physical security, and most organizations are not developing their own applications.

2. **How satisfied are you about this category?** Are you happy with the value provided by your Line of Business Applications?

3. **What's the need/opportunity for improvement in this category?** Does your organization have a vulnerability in a particular category? Or is there a great opportunity waiting to be taken advantage of?

---

[5] You can download this worksheet (and other tools) for free at http://Simplex-IT.com/BobsBook

Of course, we want to keep score. That's what we do. Total up your score, and divide by the number of categories that you didn't use, "n/a" (not applicable) or "d/k" (don't know). So if your score is 42 and you answered 1 "n/a" and 1 "d/k," you would divide 42 by 12, giving you an average of 3.5 for that section.

Critical: In this section, the higher your score, the more dependent on IT your organization is. If you scored 3 or greater, you need to make sure you've invested enough in IT (especially in the categories that are either critical or support your critical needs).

Satisfaction: In this section, the higher the score, the greater the comfort level that the resources you're allocating are both successful and appropriate. If you aren't at the point where you're investing heavily in Business Intelligence (low critical), then you can be satisfied with little or no results because it's in line with your expectations. Dissatisfaction here could be you're not seeing a bang for the buck. It's a question of defining the value.

Improvement: The higher the score, the more we need to do. This is our call-to-action list. We know we need to improve these items, because they're either actually damaging the organization or represent a great opportunity.

I separated "satisfaction" from "need for improvement." Satisfaction is a quasi-soft rating. "Yeah, we should be doing more of that." "Need for improvement" is for specific actionable "we need to fix this. Our workstations are slow and some of them are crashing."

But here's the key thing. You now have homework. From this simple exercise, you now have something measurable and possibly some things you want to follow up on. Here are some sample next steps:

1. **Queasy feeling.** You answered the questions, but aren't really comfortable with your accuracy. Who within your organization (or perhaps a partner/vendor) can increase your comfort level? Sit down with them and share your queasiness. People love shared queasiness. Trust me.

2. **Don't Know.** If you don't know the answer for some categories, um . . . who does? We're not talking about having complete detailed knowledge. But if you don't have any idea of whether you're utilizing any Business Intelligence resources, how comfortable can you be with your ability to use your corporate data effectively?

3. **Low scores.** If you have a category in which you scored high on critical, and then low on satisfaction or high on need/opportunity, do you have a plan in place to address this? If not, place a bookmark here and get started. Seriously, you've identified something that's important to your business. Deal with it. Keep in mind, you don't need to solve it. You need to make sure it **gets solved.**

By going through this process, we're giving you a simple way to self-define your IT investments. A way to self-assess your comfort level (as a non-tech CEO) of your current IT status, and create an action plan to further educate yourself (and engage your IT resource). And to assess what areas of improvement (and possibly new opportunities) for IT your organization has that you may have overlooked.

You're welcome! And thanks, Arnie.

Summary:

- The definition of "what is IT" could be a book unto itself. This method of categorization is a helpful way to identify components.

8. WHAT DOES *YOUR* CURRENT IT LOOK LIKE (A DEEPER DIVE)?

If you went through the previous chapter, you've got a 30,000-foot view of your IT. Want to go deeper? This chapter will help you do this. If you're okay with 30,000, that's fine. Skip this chapter and move on. I won't shed too many tears.

For those who stuck around, I'm going to assume that you already have an understanding about the goods and services that you provide to your customers. Hopefully, you already have a handle on that. If not . . . um . . . thanks for buying this book.

For the rest of us, let's walk through the various stages and processes that go into creating, delivering, and maintaining those goods and services from an IT perspective.

First, at each stage, what (if any) is the impact that IT has? At this point, I'm not asking for an in-depth definition, just a brief overview.

Now, we've covered the definition of IT (for purposes of this book), but here's the problem. It doesn't matter what the garden-variety definition of IT is; if it doesn't help you with your business, it's pretty much useless.

You need to have a high-level knowledge about what kinds of systems and processes your organization depends upon to exist. That's not to say you need to know everything that's installed on everybody's computer (although that information should be known by *somebody*). But you do need to understand the important pieces that have the highest impact when it works (and when it doesn't).

To start, you need to get in touch with:

1. How IT *does* impact your business, for both good and ill.
2. How IT *should* impact your business, but doesn't.

The challenge with these questions is that there isn't a right answer. No matter how you ask or answer the question (and how much money you funnel through greedy consultants like . . . well, like me), you're going to get an answer that is dependent upon some assumptions and value definitions. We'll go through what I mean by that in the next couple of sections.

Ya know, I had a really hard time with the concept of helping you understand your current IT. I started with "What's the goal?" to help you, the CEO, understand what you already have in terms of IT. Okay, easy enough.

But then my Inner Geek kicked in—you know, the part that really wants to be accurate, but doesn't really care about whether or not I'm understandable. The first couple of drafts I wrote dove right into the details about systems, applications, inventories, processes, and the like.

But the challenge with that approach is if you're willing to go into that depth, you're going beyond the focus of this book (and there are better resources, including your own IT resources, to help). And the detailed approach for a manufacturing company versus a financial services organization would be very different. Similarly, a company dependent on on-site resources versus cloud-based would also be very different.

That's why I split the sections.

In the previous section, we held to a high altitude, generalities of what you have. In this section, we're going to dig a bit deeper and talk about the same 14 components of IT (from the CW keynote), but with a bit more detail. Here are the things you should look to identify (not all may apply to your situation):

Things to know about each category:

1. **Copying/Printing.** We tend to take this for granted, but there's a lot of money expended for printing. Often, it isn't the hardware itself, but the supplies (ink cartridges and the like) that are consumed. And a lot of effort is often expended on older computers printing to newer printers or vice versa.

2. **Line of Business Applications.** These are applications that are used for the specific purpose of business process or production. QuickBooks for accounting is an example. Things we want to know about these applications:

   a. **Coverage of Application.** Are all parts of the company impacted by the application (i.e., an ERP or Enterprise Resource Management application), or just a subset (i.e., an inventory management or Sales Processing application)?

   b. **Third Party or Home Grown?** Was the system developed by a third party or by your employees?[6]

   c. **Latest Version?** Are you running the latest version? If not, why not? How many versions behind are you?

   d. **Supported?** If this is a third-party app, do you have a support agreement with them?

   e. **How Healthy is Third Party?** Are they in danger of going out of business? Has their system been regularly upgraded, improved, and supported?

---

[6] The rest of the questions are based on third party applications but can be modified to cover home grown.

   f. **Customized?** Has the application been customized for your specific needs? If so, how does this impact support and upgrades?

   g. **Outage Costs.** What is the $ impact on the organization if the system is unavailable for an hour? A day? A week?

3. **Security.** A huge topic these days (and not likely to change in the near future). We've got a whole section on this topic. I agree with CompTIA's breakdown of Cyber Security into four Pillars (more on this topic later):

   a. **Products.** These are the devices, software, and services that are purchased and implemented. But then they've got to be monitored, managed, and updated.

   b. **People.** Everybody is on the front line here. Training is critical *for all employees.*

   c. **Process.** How do you perform tasks like remote access, sharing files with external resources, and the like?

   d. **Policies.** Your Policies and Procedures need to include security issues.

4. **Physical Security.** More and more physical security devices and services are being created, deployed, and supported through IT. We're talking about security cameras (for warehouses, entrances), listening devices, and more.

   a. **Are these devices secure?** If you're able to access your office security cameras from home, can anyone else?

   b. **Do these devices give an entryway into your network?** If these devices are part of your organization's network, they may allow bad guys access to your other IT resources.

5. **Internet of Things.** Non-traditional devices on your network. These devices are relatively new, and often security was not on the minds of the people designing them. Environmental controls, shop floor equipment, intelligent power strips, even intelligent toilets and cars are now using the Internet to communicate data and allow remote control. More on this later.

6. **Audio/Visual.** Nowhere is the technology revolution so in the public eye as audio/visual, and yet it does so in a seamless way. Did anyone bat an eye that Peter Cushing had a strong supporting role in 2016's *Rogue One* movie, which is set in the Star Wars universe? Mr. Cushing, by the way, passed away in 1994.

7. **Collaboration.** Boy, separate books can be written here. But we're going to do it some gross injustices by breaking it down into three sub-categories:

   a. **Corporate Phone.** The buzzword here is VOIP (Voice Over Internet Protocol). Most companies implementing new phone systems are finding VOIP is the preferred technology. Just make sure you have enough bandwidth with your ISP.

   b. **Mobile Phones.** Seriously, is there anything these things can't do? The good news is that more and more business can be done using mobile phones. If you've got a website or any social media presence, you need to make sure you take into account how they show up on the small screen of a mobile device. You also have to consider security. If you have employees doing critical business on their phones, how do you know they don't have malware (of which there's a lot written for mobile phones) or are sending unsecure data on an unsecure wireless network?

c. **Everything Else.** How many of us have developed documents by committee where we send copies and update via email? And then somebody has to take different updates sent by multiple people and put them together . . . not any more. The ability for a group of people to work on documents and projects together has increased significantly. Whether people meet online and work on the document "side by side" from across the globe, or automatically see the latest updates, with annotations, there are lots of options, including document and change management, with approvals, comments, versioning. Good stuff. These technologies aren't just for projects involving your company. Inviting other project stakeholders (customers, vendors, etc.) is easy.

8. **Disaster Recovery.** I prefer the term "Business Continuity." And yup, there's a separate section for this one, as well. We want to answer the question, "What do we do if <fill in the blank happens>?" But for now:

a. **Backup/Recovery.** The final solution to all IT problems is "restore from backups." So it should come as no surprise we've got a section on this topic. In the meantime:

i. **Is everything important backed up?** If it ain't backed up, you ain't getting it back.

    ii. **Tested?** If you haven't tested your backups, you don't *have* backups. You *hope* you have backups.

    iii. **Remote backups?** Is your backup data stored off site?

    iv. **Protected?** A lot of ransomware and other malware targets backups.

b. **Business Prioritization.** What Business Processes have the highest priority in terms of restoring services?

c. **Single Points of Failure.** Are there specific pieces of equipment, services, or personnel that have no replacement in case of failure?

d. **Outage/Recovery Costs.** What's the cost of an hour of downtime? A day? What's the cost of recovering an hour of lost data? A day?

9. **Office Applications.** For this category, we're talking about tools that users rely on to do their job, but aren't specific to your business process. Some examples include Office Automation (Microsoft Office), Collaboration, Communication, Product Development (i.e., AutoCAD or Photoshop). Things we want to know:

a. **Product Versions.** Boy, I can't tell you how often we find companies that have four different versions of Microsoft Office, five different versions of Adobe Acrobat, and four different versions of Windows and can't understand why things don't work the same.

b. **Latest Version?** Are you running the latest version? If not, why not? How many versions behind are you?

    c. **Licensing Model.** How are you paying/buying new licenses?

    d. **Is There a Standard?** This is especially true for tools like file sharing and the like. Not having a company standard makes it difficult to support (and manage) the applications and services, from a security standpoint, as well as a productivity one.

    e. **Outage Costs.** What is the $ impact on the organization if the system is unavailable for an hour? A day? A week?

10. **Network Infrastructure (plumbing).** Data constantly flows between devices inside an office through an organization's infrastructure. It then moves through the Internet to its ultimate destination (whether it be your own cloud resources or the networks of a customer, vendor or service) through your Internet connectivity. We're going to take a real high-level view here. We just want to know:

    a. **ISP (Internet Service Provider) Info (at each location).**

        i. What kind of Internet connection do you have?

        ii. Is there a second (failover) connection?

        iii. What's the connection speed?

        iv. Monthly cost?

        v. Is it reliable?

        vi. When does the agreement expire?

        vii. Outage Costs. What is the $ impact on the organization if the connection is unavailable for an hour? A day? A week?

b. **Internet Connection Devices.** These are devices that control/maintain the connection between your location, and the rest of the world and have an increasingly important role in security. Often referred to as Routers or Firewalls, although a new term, "Unified Threat Management" (or UTM) device, is catching on strong.

  i. What kind of UTM devices do you have?
  ii. Is there a second (failover) device to be used, hopefully automatically, in case the first one fails?
  iii. Does the device include full up-to-date security services?
  iv. Age of the device?
  v. Outage Costs. What is the $ impact on the organization if the connection is unavailable for an hour? A day? A week?

c. **Switches.** These devices control the communication between all of the networked devices on your network (including computers, wireless connections, phones, printers). I don't want to dive too deeply into these, but a couple of things you want to know (more on this stuff later):

  i. **What's the speed?** This is how much data gets transmitted on each node on the switch. These days it's normal to see 1GB (one billion bits of info, with each bit being a "1" or "0"). Older switches were 100Mb (100 million bits, or 1/10 the speed).

      ii. **Is this a Managed Switch?** Most switches can be managed or optimized for your organization.

      iii. **Is it Managed?** Just because it *can* be managed doesn't mean it *is* being managed. This is especially important if you have a Voice Over IP or VOIP phone system.

  d. **Wireless Access Points.**

      i. Speed

      ii. Accessibility

11. **Hardware.** The stuff that have blinking lights.

  a. **Inventory.** Do you have an inventory of your owned and leased devices? Is it accurate? How frequently is it updated?

  b. **Warranties.** Do you have manufacturers' warranties in place for all critical devices? When do they expire?

  c. **Replacement Strategy.** How long do you expect IT equipment to last? Do you have a realistic budget in place for replacement?

12. **Cloud Computing.** More and more resources in the IT world are offered through the cloud by vendors as services, instead of purchases. Usually, they manifest themselves as monthly or annual expenditures.

  a. **Inventory.** Do you know how many services you're currently subscribing to?

  b. **Stability.** Are the vendors who are providing the services stable?

  c. **Backups.** Often the responsibility of backing up data falls not on the service provider, but the customer.

13. **Application Development.** Sometimes an application that you can purchase doesn't do everything you need to do. You need to develop your own application. Often, these applications interact with other apps. You might use a purchased accounting system for your bookkeeping, but develop your own web-based application because your product develops custom documentation as part of your product offering. See Line of Business apps for the questions here.

14. **Business Intelligence.** One of the most underutilized resources in the SMB world. There are many inexpensive (several are free) tools that utilize about the same skill level as an advanced spreadsheet. Some of the key questions:

   a. **Application Data Sources.** What kinds of data do you have as a result of all of your systems? Do you have access to them?

   b. **External Data Sources.** Are there other sources of data that would be helpful? Census data for exploring new territories?

   c. **Identified Internal Champions.** These toolsets take some investment (mostly of time and patience). Look for a couple of people to get started using these toolsets and encourage them to share their experiences with others in your organization. Or bring in a third party (uh, Simplex-IT, anyone) to get things started. But make sure a significant goal is to get some of your people started using these tools!

I want to add two more categories, both dealing with the resources you have to deal with the above issues, challenges, and opportunities.

External Actors. Third parties often provide critical IT services to their customers, whether it be full strategic services, network management, database expertise, etc.

    d.   **Inventory.** Do you have a list of all IT vendor relationships?

    e.   **Stability.** Are the vendors who are providing the services stable?

    f.   **Customer/Partner.** Do you need to have a Customer relationship (where they provide an almost commodity service) or a Partner relationship? A Partner relationship is usually more expensive, but there's a higher value on the relationship and the services that involves particular understanding of your organization and its needs. This is especially true if the vendor is providing complete or near-complete IT services (as a Managed Service Provider).

Human Resources. People. At first, I thought they were just a fad, but people seem to be here to stay. This can be particularly tricky for the SMB world. Some of these deal specifically with IT people.

    a.   **Enough.** Like any other position, staffing needs to be sufficient to handle normal operations.

    b.   **Trained.** IT changes completely every 3-5 years. Are your employees given reason (and opportunity) to at least keep a couple of toes in the water?

c. **Business.** Do they understand what your company does? Do they know that's important? Do *you* know that's important?

d. **Incentivized.** Do they want the business to succeed? Are they paid sufficiently for their efforts (with possible bonuses for specific accomplishments)?

e. **Specialized.** Are their skills sufficient for specialized projects?

f. **Pleasant.** Are they polite; can they listen? Do your employees have any problems dealing with them (or the reverse)?

g. **Respected.** Are you treating them with the respect they deserve? After all, we've spent all this time explaining how important IT is to your business. Do your IT employees feel appreciated?

h. **Realistic.** When dealing with IT issues, do your employees take into account real-world issues, like budgets, priorities, and operational impact?

Now, the above list is a good starting point, but it's a static inventory of pieces and parts. It doesn't address what these things do (or don't do) in terms of impact on your business.

We're getting there.

Summary:

- As stated in the beginning, this is taking the metaphor in the previous chapter and digging down deeper. By now, you should be able to identify some of the critical systems, applications, and services in your organization and know how comfortable you are with your knowledge of them.

9. WHAT IS ALL THIS DATA?

Remember when we talked about Data versus Information earlier? We collect data. When we use Data (adding value to the organization), we turn it into Information through our use.

Data has potential value; Information has *realized* value.

Databases are collections (usually structured) of data. BI (Business Intelligence) is the practice of processing those databases and turning them into Information.

I don't want to turn this into a primer on databases or reporting. There are better books for that. But we do have all this data we've been accumulating. We have processes for accumulating data, and we have processes for using that data (as information). When we're trying to understand *our* IT, we have to understand (at least from a high-altitude perspective) what kind of data we have and how we can use it effectively.

But what types of data are there? I think there are four types (for purposes of this discussion):

1. **Process Data.** This is data that is gathered during the process of doing business. Payables, Receivables. Sales. General Ledger. Inventory. Customer metrics. The gathered data may be used as part of the process, or simply to measure the process for quality purposes.
2. **Product Data.** This is where the data is part of the product itself. Your product might be a feasibility study, which includes data as a result of studies your organization performed.
3. **External Proprietary Data.** This is data that you have acquired from an external source (third party, vendor, customer) that is specific to your organizational needs.

An example would be data for a product that you purchase from a supplier.

4. **External Public Data.** This is data that you have acquired from an external source that is publicly available. Examples include census information, zip codes, etc.

Information Technology (in business) is really the use of technology to help us measure and assist in the creation and production of the goods and the services we provide and consume. Often, the technology creates data that we can use in a variety of ways.

In the early days, the use of data was limited to mimic what we used to do manually—general ledger, inventory, documentation, and the like. But that's changed. Now we have so much data we can ask questions about the business process that we could only dream about even a decade ago. It also allows us to customize offerings to a dizzying level. And often the data is available real-time, making us incredibly flexible to our customers and our vendors.

Summary:

- Take a moment and think through the systems, applications, and services that your organization uses in order to process your business.

- If you could "ask that data" anything, what would you ask?

- Do you have that kind of access to the data? If so, how are you using it? If not, why not?

10. WHAT'S MORE IMPORTANT, INFORMATION OR TECHNOLOGY?

One leads to the other. When you talk to geeks, in a lot of cases, we get caught up in the technologies. Technology is cool; technology is where we can measure things directly. For instance, a hard drive is a hard drive, and a processor is a processor, and memory is memory. All of this is relatively simple information.

Information has a value when it's used. It does not have a value when it's in sitting in storage, gathering dust. Information is basically that data that we can use to help facilitate either:

   a. the delivery of the goods and services to our customers and stakeholders

—or—

   b. help us maintain and improve our infrastructure.

It's the usage of the information that truly creates the value, and the technology allows us to do that. Our job is always to create great value for the organization and customers using our IT resources.

Why am I bringing this up? Because we're in the third phase of a decades-long transition. When IT first hit the scene for the SMB market back in the 80's, the primary goal was the implementation and improvement of the technology. The business process that IT performed was pretty much the same as we did manually (general ledger, word processing, spreadsheets). The technology was the shining star. We based upgrades primarily on the improvement on the tech side of things. New systems allowed us to do more things faster (by bigger processors, more storage, more memory, faster networks). It was Information **Technology**.

Then things changed, starting especially with the acceptance and commercialization of the Internet. Technology is still advancing. New hardware, software, and infrastructure are still of interest to all of us geeks. But suddenly the tools also started providing new opportunities, new insights into our own businesses (and our customers!). We started doing things radically different than before. We started being able to analyze data more effectively and quickly. Monthly Informational insights became weekly, then daily, then in real time. Reports became influential to the immediate business operations. Decisions could be made immediately, instead of flowing up to management then back down to the trenches. During this time, we were dealing with **Information Technology**.

Over the past couple of years, we've started to change again. Everything is blurring. Data can be manipulated, consumed, and presented from many sources. Completely new service industries have evolved, replacing older industries. Can you imagine anything like Facebook or Uber in the last century (and I mean the 20th!)? Anybody remember what an encyclopedia is? And these services are primarily innovations of the use of the infrastructure and data that's already gathered.

That's not to say that technology isn't evolving. A quick look at the variety of data collecting devices would answer that question. But that's taking a backseat to the evolution of what we're doing with all of the data.

Yup, we're starting to work in the world of **Information** Technology. And in my humble opinion, it's just beginning.

Summary:

- It's not enough for businesses to simply gather data to "do the work."
- Can you mine your data to develop information that's useful to you?
- Can you mine your data to develop information that's useful to customers, thereby adding value?

11. HOW DO YOU GET ANSWERS ABOUT YOUR BUSINESS? YOUR CUSTOMERS? YOUR COMPETITION?

This is where the term "Business Intelligence," or BI, comes into play. Remember we've talked about the "data" that we have accumulated (or have access to externally).

Now comes the fun part. Now we get to use it (imagine rubbing hands together with poorly-hidden glee). We convert it into Information, making it useful.

The tools are plentiful, and often actually free. Microsoft has a version of the BI tools that is pretty powerful and free (http:// PowerBI.com).

The question is . . . what's the question? That's trickier than one might think. What question are you looking to answer? Remember that the question has to match up with the data. If you want to know something about your customers that you've never gathered, your data is useless.

Sometimes, the data sources won't be the same. You might want to relate your sales to census data to determine future expansion plans. But if the census data is by census tract, you need to relate your sales data to it (which is firmly using zip codes). It can be done, but it's tricky.

Other times, you might be using different definitions within the company. This is common, especially among organizations that are just starting to integrate their reporting and processing. The term "YTD Sales" might be based on when the sales is booked to the Sales Department, but Accounting uses the same term when the product is delivered (and hits the books).

Nothing is more eye opening than for a CEO to sit down with someone who is familiar with BI tools and review their data. Far too often, CEO's think their reports are completely dependent on the ones provided by their applications.

BI Tools is another example of where services and tools that were available (and expensive) to large enterprises are now available to the small-to-medium businesses.

Summary:

- What three questions would you ask of your business systems? How close are you to seeing the answer in your existing reports?
- What external data would create additional value? Census data? Customer data?
- What questions would you ask if you had that additional data available?

12. WHAT SHOULD IT MEAN IN YOUR BUSINESS?

Whatever you do in terms of business, if IT don't flow, your business can't grow. In this chapter, I provide you with questions to reference, no matter your industry application, on how to channel your inner IT geek in the most practical fashion. You'll be able to reference these questions and return to them to revisit the concepts we touch on when you run into questions on strategy and approach.

You want to increase the value of your organization. Okay. To do that, we want to:

a.   Deliver goods and services more quickly, more efficiently, and more effectively.

b.   Support those goods and services more quickly, more efficiently, and more effectively.

c.   Deliver *different* goods and services quickly, efficiently, and effectively.

d.   Improve the value of the external relationships with external parties (which I would include such things as cash flow through better AR/AP management).

These steps create increased value, most especially in a world where we are doing more and more business using devices, mobile devices taking the cake.

How does that happen through Information Technology? Whether it be the actual ordering, or the tracking, or communicating, or relating, or building of that relationship, IT is a great way to do that with more people without necessarily increasing the budget, the cost, or the staffing.

The bottom line is that we want to "do more with less." Keep in mind that the term "less" more often means time, not $. The quicker turnaround for almost any process is viewed as increased value.

- Blockbuster rented video tapes and then DVDs to its customers through a brick-and-mortar storefront. Then came Redbox, who did it through a vending machine. Then Netflix blew both of them out of the water.
- The largest "retailer" of product on the planet? Chinese website Alibaba, which recorded $25.4 billion in sales in one day[7]. Number of warehouses? 0. Inventory? $0.
- Largest taxi company in the world? Uber. Number of cars in their fleet? 0[8].

These are companies that took traditional service and product concepts and used technology to invent completely new markets.

---

[7] http://money.cnn.com/2017/11/11/technology/singles-day-china-alibaba/index.html

[8] But not for long. http://www.mercurynews.com/2017/11/20/uber-steps-up-driverless-cars-push-with-deal-for-24000-volvos/

13. IT AND CHANGE

A manufacturing company was proudly displaying their flow chart for developing new products where they demonstrated how the product went from inception, to trials, to marketing, to sales, to market, to customers. It was a traditional flow chart with about 30 boxes or so. I started laughing. My client asked me *why* I was laughing in the middle of a meeting, so I let him in on it.

"Howard. How are you going to do all this? How are you going to make all this work? Where's the software that's going to be developed?"

They looked at the flow chart, and nowhere did it have anything about getting the computers to process the information necessary for the new product. I pointed out to Howard this has been the problem – management didn't take into account the Information Technology components. At all. Budgets, timeframes, all aspects of implementing these products were now at risk because there was no consideration for IT. Thankfully, much to their credit, they immediately saw the problem, and we immediately set to correct the situation.

The issue wasn't the flowchart. It was the *mindset* of the four people who created it, which reflected the mindset of management. IT wasn't part of their concept of the business process, or even the business in general. It wasn't part of the problem, solution, or opportunity. It wasn't part of the *business*. Because of that, any decisions made strategically or operationally started out likely to create problems.

Business 101. If you define a business process that doesn't include a critical resource for that process, the definition loses value. The further down the development process the discovery of its omission occurs, the more expensive it is to fix.

Often, the fix is a patch or a workaround, which is simple and cheap (both in terms of money and time). But these fixes are usually short-term and often create more problems downstream. And they hide the costs of the original omission.

If a company doesn't include IT in their designs of products, procedures, processes, and mindsets, and treat it as an after-thought . . . bad things will happen. I promise.

When IT systems/processes and business systems/processes don't parallel or complement each other, there will be inefficiencies which create additional work on the human side. We've created an Amish parallel, where there has to be manual labor of some kind. It's either that or we're going to add additional steps on the technology side—the ever-popular Excel worksheet that has to be filled out before anything can be entered into the system.

Either way, there's going to be friction, and there's going to be wasted energy because the two processes don't match. Sometimes they don't match because they can't. The discovery was made too far down the process, and we have to accept the limitation. Or it's a limitation in that people don't have the time, the customer needs are different, whatever. These things should be as minimized as possible, while you're also looking to be as economic and accurate as possible in the execution of your work.

Let's go through some of the most common results.

13a. Customers expect custom solutions. We can't provide that!

Why can't we?

McDonald's is a useful framework to look at for a business process. When I was a kid, if you wanted a burger with only ketchup, *McDonald's* would purposely make you wait. They could have made it quickly, but they would make you wait because that was outside their regular assembly line, and they wanted to discourage this behavior because that increased their production costs (labor), and it decreased their profits.

Enter *Burger King*, which implemented a marketing campaign for about 10 years with the jingle of "have it your way!" with whatever you want it. It was incredibly successful because you had a company that was producing essentially the same product with the options customers wanted. *McDonald's* business model penalized the customer for this flexibility. *Burger King* didn't. Ultimately *McDonald's* saw this and gave in, then started doing the same thing. Today, can you imagine a fast food provider not giving you a tremendous number of options with your product? I can't, and I've got the waistline to prove it.

The whole idea of having a meal where you could special order something was originally unthinkable. The same thing's true with just about every company; they all go through the same reaction. If all you do is produce something with very fixed attributes and specific options, you're much closer to being a commodity: just a raw material (with some specific processing). If you're a commodity, you are your price and speed of delivery. If you can't do custom solutions, you're vulnerable to your competition who can.

Systems are a big part of this. A poorly designed system locks you into providing specific solutions, with limited leeway.

An example, from the TV show M*A*S*H:
Hawkeye: [regarding the requisition of the incubator being denied]
We're not asking for a jukebox or a pizza oven.
Captain Sloan: Oh, those I can let you have.
Henry: No kidding! Hey, those would be great on movie nights. You got any pizza requisition forms?
Captain Sloan: Just use the standard S stroke 1798 and write in "Pizza" where it says "Machine Gun."
(thank you, www.Wikiquote.org)

A simple example (and one of my favorites, I admit), but consider the additional work created by this exception throughout the process. If the process is automated, then all steps automatically created for the default "Machine Gun" have to be stopped, and all steps for the pizza oven need to be done manually.

The idea of receiving a .30 caliber belt-fed pepperoni pizza comes to mind.

13b.   We Do It by Hand, Then Enter It into a System

Waaay back when (in the mid-80's), I was working at a municipality. There was a situation where job applicants had to fill out four forms to apply for a job. Each of them had much of the same information. It was early in the IT age, but we developed one form. You entered the information from the one form into the computer, then the system spit out the four equivalent forms to a printer. We geeks were proud of the system, slapped ourselves on the back in congratulations, and went about our way, looking for the next lives to brighten with our presence.

I came back about a month after we'd implemented the system, and we found that an applicant was filling out *five* forms. They filled out the original four forms, and then they filled out the fifth form that we created. I went to the people who we created the system for, and asked, "Why are we are doing this?!" The response was that they didn't like the way the forms looked when they were printed out. They didn't like it. They didn't use it. They didn't tell us. We never followed up. We never followed up to make sure that they were using the system, and they didn't like the system because of an impression of increased complexity. We fixed the system with their input and ownership and ended up with a successful system.

What ends up happening in many cases is the IT people (geeks) don't look at the processes that people on the front end (end users) are going through. The end users don't want to change, and neither party pays attention to the other. We both end up being square pegs in round holes, doing things the way we want them done, and not paying attention to the human factor that creates a collision between the two.

13c.   Henry Ford's Nightmare

"You can have any car you want . . . as long as it's black." — Henry Ford

> *"Bite me, Henry." — 21st Century Consumer*

Henry Ford's nightmare is not just an IT concern, it's one of the driving forces in business. One of the biggest concepts behind his message was the systematic application of repetitious acts.

The implementation of the moving assembly line significantly improved productivity by doing the same thing repeatedly.

We can look at the airline industry for some additional lessons. We talk about how horrible airlines are because they nickel and dime you and add everything to your cost. What they've done is cut the prices to bare bones minimum, along with the amenities that go with it. Then you have the option of adding additional options (luggage, drinks, WIFI). If you don't want the options, then it's a really cheap ticket. Are they effectively communicating that perspective? Ah, no. But companies are adapting to this level of flexibilities more and more. We must be fluid in terms of our offerings, both in terms of the product and how we offer the product.

We already talked about McDonald's, didn't we?

How do organizations do this? Often, it's through IT creating that kind of flexibility.

13d.   Isaac Newton and IT

Sir Isaac Newton (1642-1727) invented . . . well, scientific explanations concerning most of what we see and observe. His book, *Philosophiæ Naturalis Principia Mathematica* ("Mathematical Principles of Natural Philosophy"), first published in 1687. I think it's the only book Netflix hasn't turned into a series. But I've always been fascinated with how true Isaac Newton's laws of motion apply to business, and it's very much applicable to IT:

First Law: An object will remain at rest or continue to move unchanged unless acted upon by force.
Translation: An organization won't change until something forces them to change.

Second Law: The effective force on an object is equal to the mass of an object times the acceleration (F=ma).

Translation: The bigger the organization, the more force is required to change.

Third Law: When a body exerts a force on another body, the second body exerts a force equal in magnitude and opposite in direction on the other body.

Translation: Try to change an organization, and it'll try to change you.

13e. Pulling Vs. Pushing

One of the concepts that's changed dramatically is how customers receive their information, goods, and services. There's *pulling*, which is where the customer pulls the information to themselves, versus *pushing*, where the producer of the information or services pushes the information to the customer.

Newspapers are the best example (for me). Years ago (okay, we're talking even before *my* lifetime), newspapers would publish whenever the news warranted it. You could have a newspaper that was published several times a day, once a day, several times a week, or weekly.

Customer A only wants a newspaper when there's something going on that interests her. She would go to a newsstand or a drugstore and buy the newspaper, essentially *pulling* it to her. The customer defines when she wanted the information.

Customer B wants the newspaper whenever a new edition comes out. Whenever the newspaper prints a new edition, it *pushes* that product to the customer, delivering it to her home.

Same product. The difference may sound innocuous. However, it's huge because the vendor is creating information/product, but the customer decides *how* they want to receive that information.

Social media often works the same way. I can subscribe to a Twitter account (like Simplex_IT . . . I'm just suggesting) to automatically push updates to my phone because I'm terribly interested in their really, *really* interesting stuff.

If I'm only mildly interested in the topic, I can subscribe to the same Twitter account but just view it online when I choose to view the information, essentially pulling the information.

The same thing works for websites, blogs, podcasts, YouTube channels, eNewsletters . . . the more options we can make easily (critical to be easy) available to our customers, the better.

Today's IT consumers get to decide how they want that information set. This is part of the experience, and it's a core concept to IT.

13f. But that's Not the Way We Do Things!

"The most dangerous phrase in the language is 'that's not the way we do things.' "

—Admiral Grace Hopper

A lot of revolutions have happened over the years. The Industrial Revolution and Agricultural Revolution both come to mind. They happened over generations and usually spread geographically over years (if not generations). The stress within a family would be evident. A father would be on one side of the fence; the son would be on the other. Today, everything is accelerated, especially the speed of change itself. By and large, as a species, we hate change. *We hate it.* Introducing change into an organization is no different. There's resistance, and it's not light. There are two huge challenges that go into it. We're talking WIIFM and NIMBY.

1. **WIIFM.** *What's in It for Me.* If people don't see direct improvement to their way of life or their line of thinking, you're not going to get great buy in.
2. **NIMBY.** *Not in My Backyard.* An oldie but a goodie. If someone sees a change to their norm, that's going to bring a negative connotation, no matter what else is happening with what you're working to bring to the table.

When you apply these underlying emotions, it's not hard to see how easily the very thought of change is dicey to manage, mitigate, present, and pitch.

If people believe they are part of the solution, that they have value to contribute, their needs are respected, there is going to be some level of attention, cost, and investment to their well-being, they will be much more likely to accept change.

For example, let's approach the sales team so we can save the accounting department 20 hours a week. If we add 15 minutes a week to the workload of the sales team, by and large, you're going to have a hard sell no matter the benefit to accounting. Find an additional feature or benefit that's going to do *something for them.* Now you've presented the suggested change with a mindfulness to human nature. It's an absolute mistake not to consider this. Put yourself in their shoes.

13g. Beware the Boiling Toad

A toad is a cold-blooded animal. If you put a toad into a pot of water at room temperature, the toad is happy. Now put the pot onto the stove and raise the temperature to a boil. The toad won't recognize the change in temperature and will sit happily (thinking happy toad thoughts) as she boils to death. On the other hand, a toad tossed into a pot of boiling water will immediately recognize the danger and desperately try to get out.

Does your organization have a toad's approach to IT?

Common scenario: the company hasn't changed the technology in 20 years. They're using software that was good 10 years ago. It's out of date. Obsolete. But everybody knows how to use the technology, and they're successful enough. As time goes by, more and more systems fail, or they don't have the functionality that the rest of the world (and their competition) has. But that's okay, because it works just like yesterday . . . and just like tomorrow.

They bring in a new employee. She looks around and asks, *"What are you doing with all these dinosaur systems? I don't know how to use any of this stuff."*

People get comfortable with the "business as usual," as do organizations. When you bring in somebody from the outside, they often immediately recognize the shortcomings, the problems, and the challenges with the older technology. Because they've seen it elsewhere. Part of the challenge is that companies who haven't changed for a long time haven't adjusted to new realities (whether the change originates from technological advances, maturing customer needs, or new competition). Or they've adjusted in inappropriate and inefficient ways, and don't know it until somebody from the outside points out the massive issues with the rising temperature. Which is then resisted by the very nature that someone is audacious enough to point out needed change, that very uncomfortable zone outside the status quo of routine. Truth be told, sometimes the outsiders are just plain wrong. Either way, it becomes a clash between status quo (fighting change) and the newcomer (bringing in change).

Surprisingly, there are a lot of toads in the IT world. In many cases, their organizations have not allowed their IT employees the freedom to learn or implement new things. Or they plateaued and reached their comfort zone. It's part of their nature. They don't realize the obsolescence, because it still works. It still produces the same thing it has for years. There are incremental changes in terms of complexity and in terms of the solutions, with many blindly working around problems. They're *used* to it. They don't even feel that they're stewing in a pot toward their own demise, though that end may take years.

Summary:

- IT needs to be considered when planning changes to your business.
- Customers want options when they're making purchasing decisions.
- Customers also don't want complexity. The options need to be as seamless as possible.
- You may think things are automated, but are there parts that are still done by hand for all the wrong reasons?
- People fight abrupt change, unless there's a compelling reason that they can identify with to embrace change.
- People don't notice gradual change, even if it's detrimental to them.

14. WHEN IS YOUR IT OBSOLETE?

This is an ever-present challenge. The definition of obsolescence is subjective to you (the CEO); it's subjective to your workers, to your customers, and to your vendors. As I've said before in the manufacturing world, I'm convinced that the primary definition of obsolescence is "Does it turn on?" If it turns on, it's not obsolete. Whereas others, especially geeks who are on the "bleeding edge," have the definition "If it works, it's obsolete."

The truth is most companies and most organizations are somewhere between. The world is full of companies and organizations that found a sweet spot that "worked" and stayed pat. Many of these were industry giants, including several in IT. Back in the early 80s, *Wang* was the leading word-processing corporation. They had the market cornered on word processing software and equipment. *Wang* could have easily transported their word processor to the PC. They would have cornered the market on computer-based word processors. They chose not to, because it would have competed with their own product. Enter *Word Perfect* (and a bunch of similar products). Exit *Wang*.

Similarly, *Lotus 1-2-3* spreadsheet program software had the dominant spreadsheet, while the database program *dBase III* had the database world. And *Word Perfect* hesitated migrating their product to the Windows environment. These were the vendors with absolute total locks on their technologies who decided to hold back on updating because their stuff really wasn't obsolete, and they didn't want to compete with themselves. Similarly, you have organizations where the stuff still works. But the competition can do the same product and be more efficient and/or add additional options or functionality.

Can a customer have a relationship with your organization the way they want to in terms of ease of product research, placing orders, tracking progress, communication and support? You can have something that works very well for you, but if it's not evolving to match your customers' needs, you can be obsolete, even though you know your stuff works.

14a.   Stuff Still Works . . . Kinda

Some organizations feel that squeezing every last day out of IT equipment is a useful strategy. That's great, as long as you recognize the risks:

- Older equipment won't be supported by vendor warranties or will be very expensive.
- Older software isn't supported by vendors.
- Older systems don't have new features.
- Older systems consume more energy.
- Older systems are harder to centrally manage.
- Older systems don't integrate as cleanly to newer systems.
- Older systems are usually less secure.
- Younger employees will need training on old systems.
- Harder to get spare parts.
- Harder to find qualified techs to maintain.

Versus the benefits:
- I'm getting an extra year or two out of the hardware/software.

14b.   My Team Doesn't Want to Learn New Stuff!

Don't like learning new stuff? Wow, you were born in the wrong time. Change in technology is the norm, and it shows no sign of slowing. It permeates through all aspects of business and life. Once again, you ain't seen nothing yet. One of your challenges is that you have to create an environment where learning, adapting, and adjusting are part of the job. Now we're talking about culture within an organism, and that mission is a slow, slow process—and not for the faint hearted! Alas, it is absolutely critical. If you're looking to develop an organization that effectively uses IT, you have to have an organization that learns—that tries new things— and honestly, sometimes fails. I've worked with several organizations where the culture is that employees either have to learn on their own "time and dime" or they have to hide while they do it. Or where learning is limited to "Hey, we sent you to that one-day training class three years ago!" This has to change.

Aim to learn some of the newer ways to do things, and see if it's appropriate to implement. You know what your goods and services are. Investigate new or adjusted ways to create or support them. There are so many new ways to do that. There are an extraordinary number of resources that are available, both free and reasonably priced, these days to help people learn new things.

Look for champions within your organizations. People who are new to your company bring their experiences and ideas. Take advantage of them, and partner them with long-time employees within your organization to brainstorm new ideas.

You want to facilitate a good feeling or good vibes, for lack of a better word, and you want to create an environment where new stuff is cool, not threatening. Set the expectations so that your employees can actually like learning what they've been tasked to do. *You've got to heed the human factor.* Much of implementation is having an awareness of the emotional environment you create and maintain. Remember NIMBY and WIIFM. Ignore them at your own peril.

14c. I Don't Trust the Cloud

I'm still talking occasionally to potential customers who say, "I don't trust the cloud. I don't think it's secure." And these folks have networks that are often incredibly vulnerable, both in terms of security and in terms of backups and system protection. But it's *their* network, on *their* property, and this gives them a (false) sense of security.

Unfortunately for them, there's little choice moving forward without a large investment. The cloud is a large reason that SMB companies have so many options for IT improvements at relatively low cost. These companies can offer these systems and services with a single investment of equipment, software, and support services that's scaled to support their entire customer base. And they pass the savings on to you!

In terms of thinking about the cloud, there's a massive amount of security designed into that technology (when we're talking about responsible vendors). But the perception is this is less trustworthy than a company storing their backup tapes in the trunk of a 2009 Buick. The bottom line is that the technologies *are* reasonably secure, *if* they're implemented properly. It doesn't matter what the technology is or if it's cloud based or on premise. If we have somebody who has a poor implementation of local computers and local services, versus a well implemented cloud-based technology services network, the cloud will be more reliable. Now if they have a poorly implemented cloud, versus a well implemented localized storage, the reverse is going to be true.

In a nutshell, if it's done well, it works well. If it's done poorly, it works poorly. It doesn't matter what the technology is.

14d.   Geological Dig of Software and Hardware

When we visit organizations that have been around for a while, it's not unusual for us to find all sorts of hardware and software from various times. We refer to these sites as "geological digs." There are fits and stops where IT resources were purchased because there was no grand strategy for upgrading their Information Technology. Instead, when they grew, they would add some stuff. When the equipment went bad, they replaced it and so on.

Every time they had to do something with IT, their actions were totally dependent upon what was going on at the moment. Nothing was thought over; there was no grand strategy for implementing the technology. You could literally see they bought four computers from Vendor A in 2011, then three computers from Vendor B in 2012. They buy more computers from Vendor C in 2014, and they never upgrade anything. They had several different versions of *Microsoft Office*, and different backups and different anti-virus platforms. Servers were on different platforms. You could see a pattern where stuff was bought from year to year. Part of our challenge is to try and interpret this history.

Yet, everything is expected to work together, and often an incredible amount of time is spent trying to make everything work together, but this cost is hidden. Old workstations connecting to new servers (or vice versa). Free or cheap security products, with constant cleaning of malware and viruses. What we do in these situations is try to introduce an overall strategy, with the overarching approach that if at any time we need to add a computer, we know how we're going to do it. We know how we're going to configure it. And as we move forward, we adapt to change. It takes a little bit of a set up in terms of mindset and strategy, but not as much as you think. Then it becomes easier to manage and maintain.

14e.   When Do We Upgrade?

IT hardware and software are both constantly updated. When we look at the property life cycle for IT devices, we usually break it down to servers versus workstations versus devices. Some thoughts:

- The older a device is, the less likely the original vendor will support it (especially for infrastructure devices like switches and UTM's).
- Servers are critical. We keep them on the original manufacturer's warranty and replace them when they're off the warranty (or buy very expensive extensions).
- Workstations (desktops and laptops). We don't extend the warranty (unless they're critical, like CAD stations).

I recommend you have a strategy for replacement and stick with it.

For Workstations:

1. **Replace all workstations as a single project every X years.** If you have a company with 50 workstations and the goal is to get as much value out of them as possible (so X=5), every 5 years, 50 workstations are purchased.

2. **Replace workstations spread out annually over X years.** Same example as above, but the replacements are spread out. With the same 5-year plan, each year we're replacing 20% of the 50 workstations, or 10.

3. **After the warranty expires, replace them when they break.** This may seem like the "cheapest" way to do it, but not really. When it's time to replace workstations, it's an unplanned event, which is never efficient in terms of time and productivity.

Servers and Infrastructure Devices:

First of all, these are the devices that are hardest to replace and provide the greatest interruption of service when they break. So you need to:

1. **Keep them under warranty.** Keep them under the original manufacturer's warranty (or something comparable) and know what your vulnerability is (see the section on Business Continuity). How long it takes to replace, and what the operational cost is for interruption of service.

2. **How far behind?** It's one thing to be a release or version behind—much more and you're asking for trouble. Have an annual (if not quarterly) review process for your servers and infrastructure devices with your IT support. These replacements should be planned months in advance.

Summary:

- Obsolescence is not cut and dry.
- Obsolescence can't be simply defined by "does it still work well enough?"
- Have a strategy for upgrading.
- There are many hidden dangers of obsolescence.
- Maintain manufacturers' warranties for operationally critical devices.

15. CEO WHINING POINTS

As I've mentioned before, I've talked to a lot of management folks—folks in charge, folks with primary responsibility for some (or all) aspects of an organization. For conversation purposes, we're going to dump them all into one title: CEO.

There are a bunch of comments/wishes/wistful solutions/bellyaches/insights that I've heard.

Let me stress, these are sharp people. Smart. They know their stuff.

I'm also going to call on my childhood friends, "Goofus" and "Gallant" from *Highlights* magazine. These two young rascals would illustrate the wrong way of doing something (aka the "Bob" way) and the right way of doing something (aka the way my wife, Julie, wishes I would do it). I'll relate the initial anecdote as "Goofus," we'll then discuss some of the issues, and I'll return and discuss the "Gallant" way of doing things. Hopefully, by the end of the book, you'll notice a pattern of planning and process that can prevent a lot of challenges to your organization. If you also find yourself being really chafed at how annoying "Gallant" can be, I absolutely agree with you.

IT Should Just Work!

Goofus: "I don't know what the problem is. We've replaced workstations. We've upgraded servers. We moved to the newest application. I sent people to training, and still we have nothing but problems with our systems. They're slow, there are tons of errors and everybody's pissed."

Here's the fun part of Goofus' dialog. He starts by admitting he doesn't know the problem, then outlines all of the actions taken *without knowing what the problem is.*

A man is walking down a country lane. He comes upon a barn with numerous targets painted on it. Each target has an arrow right in the center—a bulls-eye for every target! Impressed, he sees a kid leaning against the barn, with a bow, an empty quiver, a can of paint and a brush.

"I'm impressed," he tells the kid. "How did you get so good that you managed to hit each target right in the center?"

"Easy" the kid smirked. "Step one, let loose the arrow. Step two, paint the target around where the arrow stuck."

IT doesn't "just" work. It's a complicated process, involving integration of multiple services, products, technologies, skills, vendors, schedules, priorities, and metrics. Too often, it's viewed as the red-headed stepchild. We'll throw some money (sometimes a lot) at it and hope (or expect or demand, doesn't matter) for the best.

Sadly, it'll never work that way, especially if you're integrating it into your organization. You have to give IT attention. You have to make it a priority in terms of ensuring that the systems and processes are appropriate in terms of cost, *value,* and complexity. And you have to buy into the metrics that make that determination.

This is especially true if IT has been ignored for years, or dealt with situationally without real thought. You might think you've been handling IT properly all these years. And you've got the bills to prove it! Unfortunately, if all you've been doing is spending money on IT, and not time . . . you're in trouble.

Think of all the stereotypical movies where the parent pays no attention to the kid, but spends a lot of money on them. Let's fast forward to the gooey part where the parent discovers the error of their ways. . .

Dad: *"I'm so sorry, Son . . . I thought that replacing all your workstations and servers would make you happy!"*

Son: *"No, Dad . . . I just wanted you to be part of my life. To show an interest . . . to guide me and make me a better IT, I mean, son!"*

Dad: *"But . . . but that's where I went wrong. I hired people to improve you and figured that's all it took to be a great CEO . . . I mean, dad."*

Son: *"But Dad, they needed to know from you what you needed and wanted me to be! Otherwise, I had no guidance. No role model. And I did some things that we both regret."*

<now you can reverse the special effects, but add some sweeping music, credits, and the like>

Okay, screenwriting isn't in my future. But you get the idea. Management by Abdication is a horrible management style, but it happens all the time in the SMB market.

Often when we first look at a new (to us) organization, we see what I call the "Geological Dig" of IT (we discussed this before). This is when we can see where an organization added pieces or layers of technology at various points without a real structure or strategy. Some examples:

- One department has a bunch of Dell desktops that were out four years ago.
- There are several standards concerning IT. Unfortunately, many are ignored or directly contradict each other.

- You can see a trail of updates, with different departments having Office 2007, 2010, 2013, 2016.
- Servers have different operating systems, versions of SQL database. Some are desktop, others installed in the rack.
- There are three different versions of backups, some to rotating disks, others to cloud.
- Some systems are patched, others, not so much.

Gallant: *"We expect workstations to last 4 years. So we budget for replacing 25% of them each year. When our users complained about having to navigate through a bunch of screens to do their jobs, so we bought second and, in some cases, third monitors. Plus we consolidated some of the application data to show up on fewer windows, simplifying things."*

IT Shouldn't be this Hard

Goofus: *"Every time I ask a simple question, the IT people have to speak four volumes of War and Peace to answer it. And it's still not an answer. I want the programs to do what we need for the business to survive. And it needs to work. I don't want to have to look at upgrading equipment, programs, and training people every time I turn around. I don't have time for this. I've got a business to run."*

Oh, woe is Goofus. Goofus has at his fingertips more tools and capacity for running his business effectively than was conceivable even five years ago. And this technology can impact his organization on every level—product, process, employee, security, quality assurance, accounting, disaster planning, future planning and forecasting. You name the level of process within the organization, and IT is there, whether you want to admit it or not.

Plus, it's growing. It's continuing to advance, not only in its capacity, but in the complexity. The same application that two to three decades ago simply meant quicker accounting reports can provide a dizzying array of insights into (again) all aspects of the organization. And it can do so with the click of a mouse button.

If it's set up right. And if it's maintained. And if you don't treat it like it's a red-headed stepchild.

Here's the thing you need to get through your head. Technology is complex. As a business person, you can't declare by edict how complexity impacts you and your organization. Every facet of technology you introduce into your organization increases the layer of complexity. If it's implemented properly (and maintained, as well), then the complexity is managed, controlled, and the negative impact is minimized.

Let the complexity run amok? Not good.

Gallant: *"Whenever we consider a change to our business offerings or processes, we specifically investigate what impact IT has, for both good and ill. The same thing when we see a significant change in technology. We ask what is the impact on business. I can't afford to get blindsided on this. I don't have time for that. I've got a business to run."*

Why Does Everything Change so Fast?

Goofus: *I'm saving money. I'm still running Windows XP on my workstations, and we're using Office 2003. I'm having some problems getting to some websites, so we bought one new computer that's over in the corner. Whenever we need to do banking or something important, that's the machine we go to. We're having some problems because some of the documents our suppliers or customers send us aren't editable on our systems, but they usually resend it in a format we can at least print out. And we can't use a lot of the newer printers, but we can usually find stuff easily enough on eBay! Yup, saving a ton of money.*

Simple answer: *Because it can.*

Not enough? Okay. A couple decades ago, somebody said it to me best. The definition of obsolescence in IT is *does it work?* If it works, it's obsolete. Why? There's such an easy entry into the IT services world, especially with cloud and software as a service. For anyone who has a new idea of delivering software or delivering services or delivering goods, the entry point is significantly less. Which means everybody has incentives to get new stuff out there. *Fast.* And there are few barriers for the market itself.

Everybody has heard of Moore's Law, named after Gordon Moore, the co-founder of Intel. In a nutshell, it states that computer processing power doubles approximately every two years. It was originally measured as the number of transistors that were contained in an integrated circuit.

My first programming job was creating applications (really just programs) on computers that had 4K (4,000) bytes of memory. There was no hard drive, no floppy drive. No graphics. No network. No connectivity. The programs were stored on audio cassettes.

So the applications were extremely limited. There's only so much you can do with only 4K of memory (I'm writing this on a tablet with 2 million times that memory).

For a good long time, all of the improvements were simply ways of doing the same thing, but faster. The CPU, memory, disk drive, network card, communication speed between devices and networks . . . just bigger, stronger, faster—and for the same price (or even cheaper).

Fast forward to today.

At first glance, the IT market looks controlled by a few vendors (Google, Microsoft, and Apple being great examples). But for every vendor who seems to control the market, there are literally hundreds of other vendors who have a thumbprint in that market.

The field is incredibly easy (relatively speaking) to jump into. Often, this is upgrades to existing technologies. Other times, it's a new offering that changes or improves (in theory) on existing offerings.

Remember our conversation about complexity? It's applicable here, as well. All of the vendors that make up our IT world potentially increase the complexity of connectivity and productivity.

Starting point:
"Hey, let's add these graphic cards for our CAD workstations! Their processors will help render drawings two to three times faster than the older graphic cards we were using!"

Two months later:
"Hey, we can't upgrade to the latest version of Windows for the CAD stations. The device driver software for the graphics card doesn't work on that."

Two months later:
"Um . . . We can't use our collaboration software on our CAD workstations because they don't have the latest version of Windows."

So, was it a bad idea to use the graphic cards? It depends on the value that those cards added (especially versus alternatives) as compared to the value that the collaboration software brings.

It's absurdly easy to add new services and add new features. Part of the challenge is that some organizations get caught up in this never-ending cycle of upgrade, simply because they need to have the latest and greatest version. But does it necessarily add value to the organization?

Right now, entering the workforce is the first generation of people who grew up on information technology. The rest of us are old farts, such as yours truly. The technology that I grew up with didn't change very dynamically until my brain (such as it is) was pretty much wired. The perception of the IT world for my generation versus the kids who grew up with IT and are entering our workforce today are very different. They don't think of things the same way we do (and I say thank goodness for that). A lot of people will automatically assume that that means they're lazy, or shiftless, or irate. I assure you, they are not (well, no more than our generation was).

Once again, we bump into matters of perception, with this conversation dialing into the convergence of generational divides between technology trends flowering out into the larger human factor between IT geek and CEO culture. The disco generation IT geeks of my era that became today's CEOs are often very upset with the millennial IT geeks. It's a particularly bad habit for the seniority to dismiss the real anatomy of what's happening, all because they don't know, or don't see the contrast.

Part of the "laziness" complaint is the reliance of the Internet to "solve all problems." "Kids today think Google has the answer to everything," I've heard stated now and again. Just like I heard adults complain about my generation when we used a calculator (my old TI-58) to calculate logarithms. "You don't appreciate math unless you calculate the value yourself," I was told. Years later, I actually heard a teacher promote required training in Assembler language (which at that point accounted for about 0.0005% of all programming jobs) because "it builds character." I wish I was kidding with that example.

I want you to see the invisible jiu-jitsu, to give you tools of understanding and uncanny perception. You're going to deal with what appears to be completely different mindsets separated by age, culture, experience, and training, hopefully working for similar goals and working together day in and day out. When we look more carefully into the sweet science in our field, it's more than just knowing tech. It's also feeling and intuiting how your internal team is working together and perceiving their interactions. Part of your job as a CEO is to power the clockwork of your organization with the most efficient amount of electricity needed.

It's tension management. Understand their fears, and know what your desired tension is, how to maintain it, and adjust when there's too much, or too little. When you dial this philosophy back to the rapid pace of change, you can get comfortable with whatever is shooting out of the curl of the pipeline. Just don't get *too* comfortable.

You think things are changing fast now? You ain't seen nothing yet (have I said that enough yet?). And you can't fight the tide. You can, however, learn tactics, and better understand the currents and unseen history behind what's creating them in the now to better manage your tomorrow.

Gallant: *"Every year, we define our IT upgrades and replacements for the next 12 months. We review that plan quarterly and make sure it's integrated into our business plan for the same timeframe. We expect to replace or upgrade hardware and services on average every 4 years, so there are no surprises. We also make sure that our employees received the appropriate training and support to aid in the transition."*

Outsourcing as a Solution?

Goofus: *"We're paying a fraction of a cost by having a completely outsourced IT resource. Any time we need anything, we contact them, and they'll work on it for peanuts (as opposed to having in-house staff or one of those 'Managed Service' doofuses). Sure, there's a learning curve when we bring them up on projects, but some of these folks are pretty darn sharp! They'll implement whatever we ask them to, so we must be sure about our requirements. And it's never the same person working on our issues, so we have to explain everything all over again. Once we asked them to update our sales reports and we didn't fully define what constituted a sale. All our reports were done wrong. That took some time to clear up, but the savings are worth it!"*

To a lot of folks, the term "outsourcing" immediately invokes visions of folks on the other side of the planet, who barely speaking English, have minimal skills, and are barely able to understand the basic concepts they're supposed to be supporting.

Ahhh . . . no. Have you ever hired a consultant? Congrats, you've outsourced. Have you ever been a consultant? Congratulations, you're an . . . um . . . outsourcee?

For this section, I'm only talking about outsourcing as a way of acquiring particular technical skills and applying them to your organization. I'm not talking about outsourcing entire services (such as your Help Desk to your customers). Different topic.

The simple fact is there are a lot of absolutely fantastic resources available on just about any side or corner of this planet . . . and there are a lot of equally lame resources with the exact same distribution model.

I should confess here to be a believer in Sturgeon's Law (named after science fiction author Theodore Sturgeon): *90% of everything is crap.*

At the end of the day, what are the primary arguments for outsourcing? They usually are at least one of these points:

1. Lower cost for the same skill
2. Don't have a full-time need for the skill
3. Required skill is hard to find

Okay, sounds great.

It's pretty easy to find an outside resource that will on paper satisfy at least one of the above points. But here's the challenge - outsourcing will not have the direct understanding that an internal person will have working with your company.

Internal resources *should* understand your organization and your needs better than an outsourced resource (this coming from a guy whose company, Simplex-IT, is used as an outsourcing resource by our customers). The challenge is that if your internal IT person (let's call him Larry) does *not* engage with your business, does *not* understand your business, and does *not* look to help bridge the gap between technology and the business process, then their benefit versus outsourcing is gone.

Larry should have explicit knowledge and experience of your business, including strengths and weaknesses of the organization, personnel, and IT infrastructure. Trust and understanding.

But that's only if the organization and Larry make that happen together. If Larry doesn't bother learning about the company and the people (unfortunately, a pretty common occurrence), that's taking two legs off of the three-legged stool. And if the management (uh . . . you?) doesn't make it a priority for Larry to do it, well then. . .

This mistake honestly makes it all the easier to justify eliminating Larry's position, because he's focusing on the services that are the easiest to externally recreate at a lower cost.

Let's introduce a new concept: "Co-Managed IT." Okay, it's not a new concept (Gartner first started using the term back in 2012). But it only recently has been scalable enough for small-medium businesses (SMB's) to take advantage of it.

Co-Managed IT is a pretty simple concept from a 30,000-foot view. It's a combination of both internal and external (outsourced) resources for the actual *management* of IT resources.

Now hear this: Co-Managed IT is coming. Like everything else, it's a management implementation along the lines of "the right tool for the right job," with the flexibility of taking that pretty deep into your organization.

Co-Managed IT is a combination of internal resources and other resources being used to manage IT. There are two basic models. The first model is where you have the IT Management (CIO/CTO (Chief Information/Technology Officer in larger organizations) or a head geek in house, and outside you have the people who are responsible for maintaining operational status quo. Then you have the reverse, where you have a person on site who has the lower skill sets (but understands the organization). Externally, the third party has more strategic skills and approach.

As I'm writing this (end of 2017), about a third of the customers we deal with are following this model—which we're finding to be quite effective.

Why? For small companies to get by with a single IT person, you're not going to get someone who has all of the skills necessary. At best, you'll get a jack of all trades.

Jack of all trades can get a good chunk of the job done, but that means they can't focus on any one particular level of technology (in terms of skill set). Look at it this way. Someone who is an expert on networks is not going to be an expert on security. A DataBase Analyst (DBA) is not going to be an expert on end user support, so that one person that you have will not have the senior skill sets for items and issues that are needed if at the same time they are expected to keep the trains running.

There's a huge disconnect between the desired application, needed skill set, and human factor when it comes to outsourcing that you really should be conscious of. Remember, though, it's better for stuff not to get broken in the first place. Let's say that's the cost, plus my brain, for a second. When we want to try to get something fixed, first of all, it *should be* preventative.

Gallant: "Tom is our internal IT resource. He's been with us for three years and understands our needs and operations. But he's not experienced with a lot of our more advanced technology. For that, we rely on Simplex-IT, our IT partner. Simplex-IT and Tom work closely together. He has access to all their monitoring tools, and they're in lockstep on projects and troubleshooting. They've got each other's back, and it shows."

We're Too Small to Need this Complicated Stuff

Goofus: "Yeah, I've seen all of this fancy technology. We don't need it. I don't want that kind of complexity or cost. Our salespeople deal with our customers one on one. I don't want a computer to get between that. And if my Plant Manager doesn't know what's going on out on the floor, then I've got an issue with him, not with a computer. We use computers; we're not slaves to them."

Notice that Goofus is talking about the complexity of the applications, not the technology that lies underneath. The complexity of the technology itself should be left to the IT pros and is outside the scope of this book.

Okay, got that off my chest.

I've noticed that when someone wants the results of a system, they use the word "sophisticated." When there are too many steps to accomplish something, the same process becomes "complicated." With a great deal of the technology that we talk about, *sophisticated* is the proper term.

"Back in the day" we often wanted to talk about sophisticated security tools, business intelligence tools, cloud optimization or virtualization, —tools that have been out in some cases for 20 years, but they were extremely expensive, as well as being extremely cumbersome. We also shied away from full-grown application software, because they were cumbersome, extremely expensive, and not scaled to smaller organizations.

The larger stuff worked well for large organizations, so they would work well with the hundreds, if not thousands, of users from the standpoint that they could afford:

- Software costs (including customization and annual maintenance and upgrade fees)
- Hardware costs (including costs of backups, failover, and upgrade/replacements)
- Training (both initial and ongoing)
- Operational costs (both on the IT and application/service sides)
- Cost of organizational change (change ain't free, boys and girls)

Smaller organizations couldn't justify the costs.

Over the past five to ten years, things have changed dramatically. This charge has been led by the cloud, but it sweeps beyond that.

We'll talk later about the details, but advances in technology have been kind to the SMB's in terms of options.

There have been three key advances that bring these options to the SMB's:

- *Device/Application Intelligence.* These services and devices are significantly smarter and becoming more and more self-managing. Configuration through Wizards and GUI (Graphical User Interfaces) make it much easier. A generalist can rely (to a certain degree) upon the device to provide some of the additional knowledge/expertise. So a BI (Business Intelligence) toolset can be run with significantly less training needed for the end user.

- *Remote Management.* More and more management of IT is being done remotely, whether it be guiding an end-user through a Microsoft Word mail merge to configuring a remote firewall to have the latest settings. The key result is that the same resource can support more users/devices. That support ration significantly lowers the operational cost. So a single network engineer can support the infrastructure devices of dozens of remote sites from her desk.
- *Da Cloud.* You knew this was going to be here. The cloud has allowed extremely complex application and infrastructure solutions to be offered to customers without the high expense. Yup, you lose layers of controls (and costs of maintaining those controls), and are dependent upon good Internet connections. But the cost savings? Significant!

Gallant: *"IT is part of our business. We know our competition is constantly trying to improve their products and services, so we have to do the same. We won't implement technology just for technology's sake. But we also don't want to ignore it. Thankfully, our IT partner, Simplex-IT, is there to help us understand what's new in technology as it relates to what we do. We're always looking for ideas to improve what we provide for our customers."*

"We Have All these Workarounds"

Goofus: *"You know our main software provides the goods and materials necessary to build the new options for our products, as long as you use these three Excel sheets. Then we have a Microsoft Access database, which is used to gather the building materials. The thing is, only one person understands how that Excel worksheet works,*

and that person is on vacation. And the author of the Microsoft
Access database left a year ago. We are in trouble."

We want the button. You know . . . the button from Staples,
the business supply company. You press it and a voice says, "That
was easy."

But the button lies. It isn't easy. Never was, never will be.
Nope. Sorry, bucko.

Worse, *we're often the reason* that it ain't easy. We let things
get complicated. When something came up that our current
systems/process didn't handle, we created a workaround to make
it work. A simple workaround.

And we promised to get back to it and make it better and
more efficient.

Yeah, right.

Our current processes and systems are the sum total of our
changes. Let's take an example. We are a company, a company
that sold widgets. They came in three sizes. Then in year two,
we sold widgets that you could buy in a presentation case. In
year three, we sold widgets that the customer could buy in a
presentation case that came with an easel. The year after that,
you could buy personalized widgets. Following year? Customized the size of the widget. The year after that, the customer can
buy personal widgets with an autographed copy of the widget
by the designer. Every year an additional layer of complexity
is added to the product and/or the process of creating and
maintaining the product.

But how did we prepare and implement the support for that
increased complexity? That's the question. Often the support is
figuratively stapled to the existing process. "We're not changing
the way we do things; we're just adding this simple step."

What is often thought of as a *"work around solution"* can lead to added complexity you, as the CEO, should have some further definition on. When you add a single workaround that impacts 1% of your orders and can be easily handled, no problem. When you have 6 "simple" workarounds that now impact 30-40% of the orders and don't play nicely together? Okay, now it's a problem.

This is especially true when the workaround was created and maintained by a Content Specialist. This is a person who honestly created the workaround for themselves and made a couple of tweaks so others within the organization can use it. It's a quick fix, cheap, and seductive to management.

In the example with Goofus, we're talking about a primary system that simply cannot handle or process the options for their products without external worksheets and a database. And the only people who know about these workarounds aren't available.

So why did we add them? Simple. It's often the easiest way to add the new capabilities without a lot of thought, process, and, possibly, expense. That's understandable. The problem is that complexity is expensive. It's hard to maintain and easy to break.

Workarounds are great for short-term solutions, especially when developing the product options or verifying their market viability. But at some point, it's time to have them "join the fold," to accept their place in the processes of the organization.

This is especially true when, over the years, multiple workarounds have been created. It's easy to get duped into thinking of the immediate change as "the only change." But the truth is, it's added to all the additional changes that have been added.

Tax law. Health care rules. Microsoft licensing. All of these started relatively simple but have been made unnecessarily and mercilessly more complex by adding new pieces and parts without removing or smoothing over what was there before the changes.

But sometimes you're left with workarounds that are truly external to the existing systems. The systems can't be modified and must be left in place. That's okay. In this case, you must make sure the workarounds are documented (both technically and operationally) and made to be as usable as possible to all appropriate employees.

Your own awareness as a CEO should have a tool box to be equipped to see what's going on.

"Gallant: Whenever we add new options to our systems (or make changes to our existing products), we'll create model solutions using tools such as Microsoft Excel and Access. Once we're sure we want to maintain this change, we'll go through a process to finalize the solutions by either modifying our main systems or nailing down the Excel/Access solutions so they can be maintained and managed by our support team."

Our Stuff Breaks All the Time!

Goofus: "We run a tight ship in terms of IT costs. We don't buy into any of those monthly plans or complicated monitoring agreements. If something's broken, we'll pay for it. But it seems like we're paying somebody to fix something all the time. Why doesn't this stuff work as advertised?"

Stuff breaks. Systems fail. Bugs pop up. Bottom line is, stuff happens.

The question is, are you doing what you can to minimize the failures? Like any equipment (including the human body), not taking pains to maintain and protect it increases the likelihood of failure.

This is especially true when the system is being used for multiple purposes, with multiple "masters." If the end user of a high-performance CAD (Computer-Aided-Design) system is also using the same system for video editing, this increases the chances of problems. So, too, if the end user has local administrative rights, so she can install whatever programs she wants to on her workstation.

A lot of times, the symptoms are there (if someone looked) before they become real problems. Hard drives are low on space before they run out. Updates and patches are long available if someone would look. And we can minimize the chances of someone accidentally installing a piece of bad software.

If you looked at all of the pieces/parts that are used on all of the devices just to a simple Google search (excuse me, Bing search . . . we are a Microsoft Partner), you'd be amazed that anything in IT works.

But for the most part, it does. And pretty darn well, in fact.

In the manufacturing world, Preventative Maintenance (PM) is a fact of life for critical equipment. That maintenance needs to be performed by appropriately skilled individuals. And woe to the well-meaning employee who felt it would be a swell idea to tweak a piece of equipment just because it seemed like a good idea at the time.

Same thing for IT. A lot of the PM actions can be performed automatically, and monitored to verify that it was done properly. Then the only special attention is to the exception—to the machines that either require a special patch or update, or separate actions altogether (or a PM task just plain failed).

This is especially true when a problem isn't obvious. Systems occasionally (but too frequently) just crash. Or it doesn't work unless the end user does some additional steps. Often, an organization sees that problem as a straight expense (bring in an outside tech for big bucks, or our in-house guy is just too busy) and not worth it. After all, if we reboot it, everything is fine. It only costs that person five minutes downtime every time.

What ends up happening is we accept the subpar performance of devices of systems and processes. The aggregate effect is never looked at. They're never being monitored. There's very little responsibility.

So subpar performance becomes the norm. Just like the workarounds gain acceptance, so too does the fact that "stuff doesn't work."

Stuff should work, IT stuff especially. But there must be a dedication of time and resource (and priority) to make that happen. I'm talking to you, CEO.

Strictly speaking, much of IT is a mature enough technology so that a majority of this stuff *should just work*. And if it doesn't, I think expecting that it should be fixed in a reasonable amount of time is reasonable, if your IT resources (both the equipment and the resources maintaining them) are appropriate to the task. Let's say your organization has 50 workstations purchased from a consumer electronics store, and your server is 10 years old. Oh, and the person tasked with keeping this stuff running has 15 hours of other duties each week, with no budget for training or monitoring tools. Guess what? You're going to have problems with your IT. And some of them will be hard to discover, let alone fix, especially if we're unwilling to purchase the "right tools for the right job" in terms of equipment, resources, or services. This is a dynamic we can't avoid.

As a CEO, look to break apart the fabric of the nature of the business into its habits. You can divine wonderful ways to lessen this impact with more mindfulness to the unavoidable, while also working on the relationship between the IT geeks under your wing and the rest of your organization. They can't stop them. But they can take measures to lessen the frequency of their impact.

Gallant: I have a quarterly walk-through where we review the service tickets we had for our IT services. I listen to any recommendation about replacing equipment, and we make sure we're buying the right tools for the right jobs. I particularly pay attention to problems that happen more than once; we don't want those!

I Bought New Equipment, but It's Still Slow

Goofus: "My end users were complaining for months that our main business application was too slow for them to be effective. We finally decided to replace all of our servers with new hardware and upgraded the software. A pretty penny, but we wanted to get rid of the complaining. Forty thousand dollars later, we're a little bit faster than we were, so now we're going to replace all the desktops with the latest. That should fix it!"

Consider this scenario. A guy calls into a car dealership and asks to talk to the service manager. "Hey, bub! I bought new mud flaps for my 4x4 truck at your dealership. But the damn thing still gets the same gas mileage! AND I picked up new windshield wipers, too, but the tire pressure is still the same. I thought you people were about *service*! What gives?!"

Funny, right? Of course, we'd never be that silly. Ah . . . *well,* we often are. The guy on the phone call went ahead and replaced parts of his system (in this case, a truck) and measured success by an improved metric (in this case, two—namely, improved gas mileage and increased tire pressure). But there's no implied relation between the replaced parts and the metrics he wanted improved.

This happens a lot in IT. I call it "Ready, Fire, Aim." The easiest "big change" that can be made in IT is to simply replace the equipment. It'll probably be bigger, faster, stronger, and shinier than the older stuff. Plus, it looks like you're actually doing something, which is a plus.

But there's a disconnect between perception and reality when dealing with this type of situation. Upgrades don't always bring specific solutions to specific needs. If we don't understand where the problem that we're trying to solve is stemming from, our solutions are shots in the dark that go everywhere, hopefully including the target.

Systems require a lot of resources being allocated and consumed. For a simple application that runs on a workstation and communicates with data on a server, consider the following resources:

1. Workstation CPU (processor)
2. Workstation RAM (memory)
3. Workstation hard drive (storage) speed and available space
4. Workstation work load
5. Workstation network connection
6. Network saturation
7. Server network connection

8. Server work load
9. Server hard drive (storage) speed and available space
10. Server RAM (memory)
11. Server CPU (processor)
12. Database load (other users)
13. Database optimization (well defined)
14. Application optimization (some aspects of app receive higher priority)
15. User believes it's slow

Those 15 resources could lead to consistent performance issues for applications. There are a bunch more; I just listed the easy ones.

Replace the server and possibly fix #'s 7-11. Replace the workstations and possibly fix #'s 1-5. If the issue is #'s 6 or 12-15, you've probably fixed nothing.

Every one of these metrics can be measured, given a bit of time and patience. And every one of them has behavioral characteristics you'd expect to see when they're the bottleneck. For example, if the server is running out of memory, you'll see a lot more disk caching. Or if a SQL query isn't optimized (boy, do we see a lot of that!), we can see the number of database reads skyrocket.

Ask questions: what are the resources that are making bottlenecks, and how stressed are they? Then we can make sure that the investments we make are the appropriate ones. Develop a feel for the organic problems that may be being created on both sides of the fence.

Gallant: "My end users were complaining that our main business application was too slow for them to be effective. We spoke with them, and it turned out to be only during late afternoons.

Our IT guys monitoring the systems identified that around 3pm every day somebody was running a set of reports that could really be run at 3am. Our IT guys were able to optimize the schedule which freed up server resources during the day. Everybody's happy."

How Can I Control Costs?

"Goofus: I wish we had a budget. Every time I turn around, we have to replace equipment, upgrade it, or add. And don't get me started about everything we're paying a monthly fee for! I think these vendors invent the needs for these services. And don't get me started about the consultants. But I keep hearing we need them, so I guess the checkbook is always there."

I'm amazed at how many companies manage their IT budget as a "this is what we expect to happen," as opposed to "this is what we plan to happen."

Like all expense lines, IT has several categories that you can expect:

1. *Equipment.* Keeping the old stuff running. Replacing old stuff with new stuff. Buying new stuff that we didn't have before.
2. *Software.* Keeping the old stuff running. Replacing old stuff with new stuff. Buying new stuff that we didn't have before.
3. *Services.* Keeping the old stuff running. Replacing old stuff with new stuff. Buying new stuff that we didn't have before.

4. *Personnel.* Paying the old folks. Replacing old folks with new folks. Hiring new folks that we didn't have before.

Now, that seems a little simple. 'Cuz it is. We can (and should) make it more complex because almost all of these can be either purchased, leased, rented, or "As A Service" (it's a fancy term for rent, more on that later).

A lot of this is driven by obsolescence. We'll cover the definition of obsolescence in much more detail later. For now, let's keep it limited to cost control. Anything involving IT will become obsolete, but here's the key issue (and take this to heart):

YOU decide what is obsolete within your organization. Not the industry. Not the consultants. Certainly, not the vendors. Absolutely listen to them. But do not abdicate your responsibility to your organization.

With new customers, we try to get a feel of their definition of obsolescence with the hardware, software, and services they are purchasing right off the bat. With manufacturing customers, we often joke that "if the lights come on when you flip the switch, it's not obsolete." So they're used to buying something with an investment in capital costs up front. This new product of theirs will then be driven into the ground, which could be 10, 20, even 30 years if it can be used effectively for that long.

Not so much for IT investing, which is tricky.

IT changes. Quickly. And the costing model is switching from capital investments to monthly investments. This is a great thing if you're looking to smooth your expenses over time and avoid huge spikes in expenses. If you like buying stuff and running it into the ground, you're going to be annoyed.

This is the way many companies work with their IT infrastructure. We have a customer that bought their last largescale equipment back in the late 90s, and, for the most part, all they did was to replace a couple of PCs here and there. For the most part, however, over the last 15 to 20 years, they have not made a major investment in terms of capital IT costs. Over the past couple of years, their equipment failure rate is increasing, and their old technology cannot help them implement product and service changes critical to meet or exceed their competition. Now the good news is they got a decade and a half of quality business growth and effective use out of this. The bad news is nearly everything has to be replaced.

If they knew that's what was going to happen, their eyes are wide open. Good for them if they understand now that everything they've been using is obsolete, and there is going to be one large expenditure today. As long as they understand and this is factored into their budget appropriately, this can be just fine (although it ain't the way I'd do it).

The common model of today is to determine your expectation to refresh hardware and services over a given period of years. Usually, it's somewhere between three and five. Compare that to placing the same resources in the cloud, where you're going to pay a constant monthly fee through that same period.

You can control costs by embracing the model in which you're maintaining and improving your IT investments. But understand that there's a limited amount of time or limited amount of value you pull out of the capital investments, or it's an ongoing investment if you're going to be continuing to pay for those maintenance and improvements.

As a service model, service software, and a service infrastructure, providing a budgeted manner of paying monthly fees for these services is the foundation of where our business comes from.

Gallant: "We have a budget. And a process that annually creates that budget based on realistic expectations and experiences. And it's tied into our business plan for the upcoming year. The IT folks are responsible for only part of that process.

I Don't Wanna Understand IT!

Goofus: I don't want to understand IT.

Ummm . . . We'll talk in more detail about what you need to understand about IT. But the initial response can be summed up here:

Too bad (more later).

Gallant: I don't need to be an IT expert. I just need to understand enough so I can make informed decisions about IT and my company.

Summary:

- There are a lot of common reasons people when explaining problems in IT.
- Often there are underlying issues.
- Don't just "make the excuse." Find out what's really going on.

PART II

Geek Stuff that Impacts the CEO Side

16. BACKUPS
'Cuz Nothing Else Matters

Pop quiz time! Here are some of the IT disasters that could really muck your day. Ready?

- Ransomware hits your organization; all of your files are encrypted. Bad guys don't feel bad about it.
- Employee accidentally deleted critical files, but feels really bad about it.
- Software upgrade was applied to your line of business app. It doesn't work. Vendor feels really bad about it.
- Mountain Dew was added to server internals. IT guy feels really bad about it. So does the server.
- Power goes out in building, and your battery backups aren't as reliable as you thought.
- New data entry employee goes on a tear and enters two weeks' worth of data into the system. Incorrectly.
- Sales manager leaves laptop in a taxi. Seriously. Someone is still taking taxis.
- Top sales guy deletes all his sales contacts from his system before turning in his immediate resignation.

The question is, what's our final last-ditch solution for all these problems?

If you answered, "Update my resume," you're probably not the CEO and probably caused the problem in the first place.

The right answer (if for no other reason than it's the subject of the chapter) is "Restore from Backups," congratulations. You win!

Backups are about the most boring aspect of IT, right up there with software licensing. They don't increase revenue. They only add cost. But they're the last line of defense for almost anything that goes wrong involving IT. No matter what the problem is, if all else fails, a good backup means you're not completely screwed.

Notice I sneaked the word "good" in there? Probably 20% of the new customers we bring on board haven't had a good backup for several months. Usually, they were told the backups were good by the prior support folks.

Backups are the ultimate mulligans for companies in the sense that you get to either recover or undo some data that was either appropriately or inappropriately removed or updated. Sometimes the data was mucked up through system or hardware failure. Sometimes by malicious activity (like ransomware), or the eternal "oopsie" from an end user. Backing up all of this data is your insurance policy; and no matter what the cause, the last line of defense is your backup copy of the data or the application.

This section is focusing on making and storing the backups. We'll talk about *using* the backup in case of a disaster in the section about Business Continuity.

For purposes of this section, a backup is a set of secure, reliable, and accessible copies of data on a routine schedule. The backup set is stored on a secure and separate device or service from the original.

Although we're using the term "data," it's important to note that when backing up a device (like a server), we usually want to back up everything. The programs, the configurations, the operating system itself. If it takes up space on the server, we want to back it up (with a few rather geeky exceptions, which we'll conveniently ignore).

Why back up everything, if only the application data changes daily? It's a question of recovery time. If we don't have a copy of the programs and the configuration of the server that is now in a smoking heap in the corner, we'll have to rebuild it and reinstall and reconfigure everything. If we have a backup of *the whole server*, then we can simply restore *the whole server*.

We also need to make sure that the backups are good and that the backups are secure. And it's necessary to invest the appropriate resources.

Bob's Rules of Backup:

Disclaimer:

We're not going to spend much time on the technology behind the backups—just the business requirements that the technology needs to fulfill. But if your backup strategy has the word "tape" in it, you probably need to revisit your strategy.

1. If there's data pertaining to your business stored somewhere, it should be backed up.
2. Servers should be completely backed up.

3. All backups should be centrally managed.
4. Personal backups (i.e., thumb drives, DVD's and personal services like iCloud or DropBox) should not be allowed.
5. If you're not sure, back it up.
6. Know what's **not** being backed up.
7. If it's not tested, it's not a real back up.

Now let's ask some appropriate questions:

1. What *should* you be backing up?
2. What *are* you backing up?
3. *Where* are your backups located?
4. Are your backups any good?
5. Don't forget Cloud Services!
6. Are your backups safe?

What *Should* You be Backing Up?

What do you need to back up? If you're not sure, you need to back it up. That's your first rule of rule of thumb. With any information about your organization, your customers, and your vendors stored on a device, you need to have a copy of it somewhere else.

Backups usually fall into three categories, based on the device:

1. **Servers.** A company server provides processes, applications, security, and other critical functions. To configure a server is often a complicated and time-consuming process. We recommend (strongly) backing up all data on all drives, so the server is completely recoverable from

the backup, programs, configurations, and all. If it's stored on the server, it's backed up. Period.

2. **Local workstations.** Most workstations are pretty generic (easy to replace), except for the data. So we configure the workstations so that all data is stored on the servers (or cloud). This means we don't need to backup most workstations. The exception would be workstations that have critical or complicated roles or applications, like CAD. Those puppies we treat like servers.

3. **Remote or travelling devices (like laptops, tablets).** I like having third party applications that are business class (like Anchor from eFolder) to automatically back-up specific folders (that can be centrally managed) to the cloud. These services can also be used to synchronize files between users, customers, and corporate servers. *The key issue here is don't rely on employees to back stuff up. That ain't their job, and it shouldn't be . . . and that includes **your** laptop.*

4. **Cloud Services.** You might be paying Microsoft for your email, Google for document storage, or SalesForce for your Sales Force Automation needs, but is your data stored on their services backed up?

For each of those backups, we need to ask the following questions:

1. **How frequently do we back up data?** If we back up data every 12 hours, that means we run the risk of losing up to 11 hours and 59 minutes of data. Is that acceptable? If we want to back data up every 5 minutes, then we run the risk of clogging up the network and systems

with a lot of backup traffic. Is that acceptable? *Hint: Different systems will have different requirements.* More on this in our Business Continuity section.

2. **How far back do we need to keep backups?** Obviously, we want to get the most recent copy of our data should we have an immediate recovery need (server went down, laptop stolen). But what if we deleted a document a year ago and only today realized it was missing?

3. **How quick/easy is it to recover data?** You should be able to recover data stored on a backup within a reasonable timeframe (within an hour for most cases).

What *are* You Backing Up?

This one's on you, CEO. You need to have an idea how your current backup strategy relates to the above list. This is one of those things where if this is the only useful thing you get out of the book, it'll be worth it.

Where Should Your Backups Be?

Whether the data is stored in the cloud, stored on a server, stored on a computer, stored on a thumb drive, stored on a CD or DVD, if it's part of a fortune cookie, stored on a roll of toilet paper, on a papyrus roll, on a homing pigeon, whatever . . . it's vulnerable if it's only stored on *one* of those items.

If you have backups that are in the same building, do you have backups that are in the cloud? Do you have the backup that are in a cabinet? Do you have backups that are in the trunk of somebody's car? Do you have backups that are in the closet of someone's home? Do you have backups that are strapped to the back of the St. Bernard running through the Swiss Alps with a keg of brandy? Is it good brandy? Can I have some?

You need to know *where* the backups are located. If backups are stored in the same building as the computer (and not in a fireproof vault) and that building burned down, it's not going to be terribly useful. IT back up strategies are based on relative simple logic. Reviewing the basics never hurts.

Also, consider if disaster does strike, we need to know how long your business can afford to be without access to information, as well as what the cost of being down is (more on that in the "Business Continuity" section).

On the one side, we want to get to that backup set as quickly as possible. On the other hand, we don't want the backup to be a victim to the same catastrophe. A backup set that's encrypted by ransomware is essentially useless.

My recommendation is that server backups should be in at least three locations:

1. **On the server itself.** Microsoft Windows Server has a great feature that's far too often unused, namely Shadow Copy. It allows end users to easily recover accidentally deleted documents or folders and stores a long history of the files on the server. Introduced back in Server 2008, we frequently find it not set up on new customers (and it's really easy and free!). Want to know if you've got it? Just right click on a folder that has your documents and see if the phrase "Restore Previous Versions" (or the like) is an option. If it is, you should be good. If not, check with your IT provider.

2. **Local (part of your network in your facility).** A designated backup storage device that's properly secured but quickly accessible. These devices can be used to recover files and complete systems. Many (designated as BDR or "Backup Disaster Recovery" devices) can actually run the backups as a virtual server in the case of a complete server outage (more on that in the "Business Continuity" section).

3. **Cloud.** To protect against the scenario where the outage engulfed the entire facility (think fire or significant security breach), a cloud solution is my recommendation. Some companies have multiple locations and swap backups between them. That's certainly better than just on site, but if they're connected via a network, there's a greater risk of damage to the backup than if they're on a separate network.

Notice that I'm not talking about taking drives offsite. That's because I think that any backup strategy has to be automated. The days of relying on even trained, skilled, responsible people (so I'm automatically disqualified) to remember every week or day to swap hard drives or even tapes are long over. That's not what you're paying people for, and if you swap weekly every Friday, your company is at risk of losing up to a week of work (think bad things happening on Thursday).

Don't Forget Cloud Services

In this day of Cloud Services, it's easy to forget that data created by these services needs to be backed up, too! Many of these services only provide backups that are meant to recover data in case of recent loss, but not if a user accidentally (or purpose-fully) deleted documents some time ago. We've run into several instances where we've been contacted by a potential client that erased a former employee mailbox from Office 365 months ago and only now realized that they needed something. Too late!

If you have servers that you maintain running in the cloud (like Microsoft's Azure or Amazons' AWS), make sure you're running an appropriate backup strategy for those resources. Although a third party is hosting those resources, it's your responsibility to make sure they're being backed up.

Many of these services (like Office 365, Azure and AWS) offer additional backup options (sometimes at a cost), and third parties are sprouting up that do the same. Review your current Cloud Services and make sure you're appropriately covered.

Are Your Backups any Good?

Example #1:

A few years ago, we monitored a client's network, but another company handled their backups. There was an error involving the storage devices on their primary physical server, which re-quired a quick fix that would take 5 minutes. And it would work 95% of the time. The other 5%, it would destroy the data that was on the device. That would be bad.

No problem, we thought. The odds are 95% that it's a quick fix, and if we're unlucky to be in the 5%, we'll recover from the last backup. The client will lose a couple hours of produc-tivity, and one of our techs will have a late night, but not that critical. And the other company assured us that the backups were good.

Well, we decided to test their claim. Good thing we did. Turns out their idea of a good backup was that there were no errors. But there were no errors because they were backing up . . . well, nothing. They were backing up nothing for months and thinking things were great.

That changed everything. We couldn't risk even a 5% chance since we had no way to recover the lost data. What was going to be a quick fix turned into a 72-hour marathon of finding and moving bits of data off of the problem device until we had taken as much off as possible. The company was effectively unable to work on their critical products during this time. So the loss in terms of productivity was significant.

Finally, after pulling as much data off the device as we could, we tried the 5-minute fix. Of course, it worked perfectly. Those 72 hours of work (and down time) were completely unnecessary, but we had no choice.

Example #2

A couple years later, we had a client leave us (hey, it happens!). They couldn't afford our services, and the owner "knew a guy" who would take over managing their IT at a much lower cost. We, of course, helped with the turnover.

A little over a year later, we got a panicked call from the owner. The server suffered a failure in the drive controller, and in order to fix it, they would have to reconfigure the storage array. That would erase all existing data (which they couldn't get to, anyway). No problem, we said, just restore from your last backup (yup, we're eager to help even former customers).

That's when we were told that the backups stopped working about three months earlier. There was a problem with a daily backup that prevented the subsequent backups from working. The backups generated alerts. There were also testing jobs that created alerts. But the problem was that nobody was paying attention to the alerts.

Thankfully (sorta) we were able to engage a third party storage recovery specialist that was able to recover about 90% of the data that was lost off of the storage array.

The cost for recovery? A little over $15k, plus 4 days of down time (2 days before they contacted us and 2 days to recover). But the alternative was the company going out of business. It's as simple as that.

An untested backup simply isn't a backup. You need to know that the backups are complete *and* secure. It's great to know that you've got a history of what seem to be successful backups, and that the frequency of backups are appropriate. But if you haven't tested or recovered something from it, they're potentially useless.

Why do local fire departments visit companies and check the charge of the fire extinguishers? Why do some cities test the tornado warning sirens weekly? We've seen several instances where organizations have thought they were running backups, and that they were good backups. They thought everything was operating properly, so they never bothered to try to recover any data.

Every business-class backup solution provides good solid tests to verify that backups are complete and reliable. At Simplex-IT, we constantly monitor backups for our customers and have several layers of alerts and testing.

Are they safe?

Christian Szell: Is it safe? . . . Is it safe?
Babe: You're talking to me?
Christian Szell: Is it safe?
Babe: Is what safe?
Christian Szell: Is it safe?
Babe: I don't know what you mean. I can't tell you something's safe
or not, unless I know specifically what you're talking about.
Christian Szell: Is it safe?
Babe: Tell me what the "it" refers to.
Christian Szell: Is it safe?
Babe: Yes, it's safe, it's very safe, it's so safe you wouldn't believe it.
Christian Szell: Is it safe?
Babe: No. It's not safe, it's . . . very dangerous, be careful.
Laurence Olivier (Szell) and Dustin Hoffman (Babe), *Marathon
Man*

It's great to have backups. But you need to make sure they're
safe. By that, I mean you want them to be separate from the
device they're backing up.

Let's take a company that has a single server. They backup the
server to a removable hard drive that's connected to . . . wait for
it . . . the server. The power supply goes wonky and creates a
huge spike that hits everything . . . including the backup drive.
Server and backup are now toast.

Any backup device that's physically connected to the network
at your location is physically vulnerable to the same threats as
the rest of your network. This means a disaster is equally effective against your backup device as it is against your server . . .
bad news.

Safe also means protected from outside interference. So you want to limit access to the backups, preventing a majority of users from being able to access them. Because if a user is compromised (or just angry) and they can wreak havoc on the backups, as well as the server . . . you are once again toast.

Backups contain a ton of data (hopefully all of it). You need to protect it just as actively as you protect your other IT resources, in fact, more so. That means encrypting your backups and limiting access from employees (and monitoring access, as well).

More on this in the Security section.

But we want to have backups available locally, because if they're needed and available, the recovery time is significantly better than cloud only (if they're spared from damage). See our section on Plumbing for more details on that.

If there's a third party involved in storing your cloud backups, they should have access to the cloud backups, but not the data within the backups.

Summary:

- Just like security, your backup strategy should be reviewed by a competent IT partner. Yup, Simplex-IT comes to mind. What a shock, right?
- Backups are one of the most critical components of any organization's IT strategy.
- If it's important, it should be backed up.
- And monitored.
- And tested.
- Here's our approach to backups:
  o   On Premise devices

- Workstations. We configure the network so that all documents and a majority of user configurations (desktop, favorites) are stored on servers. Workstations aren't backed up. We recommend that our customers have a spare workstation that can be used to quickly replace a workstation in case of problems.
- Servers.
    - They are backed by incremental image-level backups several times a day to a separate device located on the network. The backups are stored in a spot that is extremely secure (only a couple of accounts have access).
    - They all have Shadow Copy configured with at least two backups per day on each drive (as appropriate).
    - Each day, the backups are pushed up to a cloud host, fully encrypted.
    - Each day, several tests are applied to each backup, the daily consolidation of backups, and the cloud host.
    - A routine test of mounting (recovering) backups is done at least monthly.
  o Remote workstations (laptops, etc.)
    - File synchronization tools (like Anchor from eFolder) are used to automatically backup key folders used by remote employees. Whatever tool is used, it needs to have the ability to be centrally managed and monitored.

o Cloud Servers

- The configuration of the cloud-based servers should include the same layer of backups as on-premise servers, although the tools to accomplish this will differ somewhat.

o Cloud Services

- Cloud services should be reviewed to understand their default backup offerings.

- If necessary, either the original vendor or a third party solution should be implemented and monitored.

17. BUSINESS CONTINUITY

*Because the Shit **Will** Hit the Fan (it's just a question of when)*

When speaking to groups, I often say, "The worst time to learn CPR is when someone is having a heart attack." My point is that reacting to an emergency without any kind of plan is extremely dangerous. A recent CompTIA paper quoted a Gartner report, saying that a business having a catastrophic data event has a two-year survival rate of 6%.[9] On the flip side, the same article quotes CDW research, showing that "82% of significant network disruptions in U.S. businesses could be reduced or avoided by implementing even the most rudimentary data recovery and business continuity processes."

In other words, disasters suck, but there are some relatively low-cost things you can do to minimize the impact. But you must take those steps *before* the disaster.

You need a plan. How detailed a plan? That's up to you. A key point to keep in mind is that this is not just about how to get your computer systems back up and running. All of your business processes can be impacted by the disaster.

Scope Matters

I'm an IT guy. This is a book about IT. So, we're mostly going to talk about IT stuff. However, disasters aren't picky. A disaster can have nothing to do with technology. That group of 10 employees who go in on lottery tickets wins big. Your biggest customer representing 25% of your revenue goes under. Your

---

[9] "CompTIA Quick Start Guide to Business Continuity and Data Recovery": https://www.comptia.org/resources/comptia-quick-start-guide-to-business-continuity-and-data-recovery

anti-virus works great on your computers, but your employees all get sick at a key time. Those are outside of the scope of this book, but some of this discussion might be helpful for those situations, as well.

Business Continuity Versus Disaster Recovery

Twenty or thirty years ago, we used the term Disaster Recovery (DR). DR started with the assumption that a disaster would significantly disrupt business operations. The DR plan would be the steps necessary to bring back operations in an orderly fashion. My first DR plan was for a city municipality back around 1985 or so, where I was the IT Manager (although it was called DP, or Data Processing, back then).

About ten years ago, a new term popped up: Business Continuity (BC). In the IT world, new buzzwords are often just a way to put lipstick on a pig and repackage the conversation to charge a little bit more money for it. But in this case, there actually is an additional value that BC has over DR. BC starts with the assumptions that the disruption to business can be minimized and often eliminated with some key investments and planning.

So what the heck is a disaster (aside from the obvious example of "Indiana Jones and the Kingdom of the Crystal Skull," of course)? CompTIA's report gave five categories:

- **Environmental.** Heat, cooling, server or network gear failure, or power failure, bankruptcy, etc.
- **Vendor**. Failure by vendors, software, communication outage, non-performance to support SLAs, etc.
- **Natural**. Earthquake, flooding, tornado, fire, etc.

- **Human**. Key employees leaving the organization, human error (intentional or unintentional), opening infected email attachments.

The second thing we want to talk about is the scope of the disaster. What parts of your organization are impacted (now we're just talking about disasters involving IT)?

- **Individual User**. Only a single person or device.
- **Specific Device**. A single device is impacted.
- **Specific Application**. All users of a specific application are impacted.
- **Facility**. Many (or all) devices on site are impacted.
- **External Connectivity**. The business location cannot connect externally.
- **Internal Connectivity**. Devices inside the business location cannot connect to each other.
- **Cloud Services**. Specific Cloud Services are impacted (managed by third party).

Scaling Your Business Continuity Strategy

Okay, let's be honest. If you're truly serious about developing a complete BC solution for your organization, one chapter in a book ain't gonna cut it. You're going to have to go deeper. The BC requirements for the parts of your company that are very dependent on IT are going to be very different than BC requirements that aren't.

So, how do you approach it? That depends on how much time you're willing to commit to developing a strategy. The plan (and need) for maintaining your internal systems versus maintaining your cloud-based systems might be very different.

This is why the risk discussion here is so critical. You need to understand both the risk of disaster and the cost of the disaster. Only then can you make the value judgement of how much resource and effort you're willing to expend to protect against disasters.

The Risk of a Disaster

We want to create a Business Continuity solution, one that's appropriate in terms of scale, complexity, and cost. One of the first questions, of course, is going to be "How much is it gonna cost?"

Business Continuity can be a simple and cheap solution ("in case of disaster, we close shop and go softly into the night") or incredibly complex and expensive (with lots of blinking lights, backups of backups of backups, and Bruce Willis, Arnold Schwarzenegger, and Jeremy Brett[10] at your beck and call.

What's the Cost of Downtime?

This is one of those conversations that CEOs hate to have, because they are required to apply it to a number to things. Let's say we have 10 people, and those people cost $25 an hour. One hour of them not being able to do their job (but we're still paying them) costs us $250.

But is that it? Hardly. Employees are there to create value to the company and to our customers. That's also been impacted. Deadlines might be missed. Deliveries delayed. Customer goodwill lost. An interruption like that has even more impact than just payroll costs.

---

[10] The absolute best Sherlock Holmes of all time.

The challenge here is that this is not a technical question. Don't let geeks drive this conversation. This is your time, good buddy of a CEO, where you **must** drive the discussion **and come up with an answer**. If you don't, you're abdicating your responsibility.

You can also break down your organization to the key components. Ask your management team these questions:

- What would happen if our manufacturing system was down?
- What would happen if our website was down?
- What would happen if our customer service lines were down?

Armed with that knowledge, we can decide how critical it is to minimize the possibility of an outage and prepare how to keep things going if one happened.

What's the Cost of Recovering Lost Data/Work?

In many cases, our solutions are dependent on data (or whole systems) that are backed up to other devices (either stored locally or offline in the cloud, as discussed in the last chapter on backups). Real-time backups are optimal. They're where entered data is immediately replicated to the backups. Unfortunately, they're usually pretty expensive and not always practical.

That leaves us with the traditional scheduled backups, scheduled throughout the work day—which leaves us a vulnerability. If we schedule backups every 2 hours, we run the risk of losing data for up to 1 hour and 59 minutes.

Think about that. How easy would it be for your organization to rebuild up to two hours of lost work? How would you define that as a cost? You can increase the frequency of backups throughout the day, although at a certain point you'll start impacting the performance of the network (your resources are working more on backing up data than in creating the data in the first place).

Again, my CEO buddy, you need to answer this question. The problem here is, I know geeks. I am one. We love to answer these questions. But this one isn't ours to answer.

Here's the magic equation, simplified:

$$\textit{Cost of Downtime per Hour} \times \textit{\# Hours down}$$
$$+$$
$$\underline{\textit{Cost of Recovering Lost Data per Hour} \times \textit{\# Hours data lost}}$$
$$= \textit{Business Cost of Disaster (BCOD)}$$

We're going to come back to this value.

5 Questions You Need to Ask Yourself (homework)

Bad things happen. We know that. We'll try to prevent bad things. (It's why God created salad bar sneeze guards, warning signs on ladders, and bubble wrap). That's called prevention. We'll also try to be ready to minimize the damage (which is why God also created spare tires, band aids, and air sickness bags). That's called containment. But we need to scale our prevention/containment strategies. Do we need more than one spare tire? Probably not, unless we like to go to "Edward Scissorhands's Car Wash and Detailing." This means that we're accepting the risk. This saves us from the expense of the second tire and gives us the additional trunk space.

Let's answer these questions. Remember the discussion we had earlier on scaling? The same conversation is true here. You can get as detailed here as you'd like. And you'll probably want to include some of your business process and IT resource folks.

For each identified portion of your business (whether it be process, department, product), you should identify:

1. **What Bad Things could happen?** For example, specific equipment failure, human error, security breach, environmental problem, loss of power, connectivity.
2. **For each Bad Thing, how likely is it to happen?** Use a scale of 1 (low) to 5 (high).
3. **For each Bad Thing, what can be done to Prevent?** Upgrade of equipment, failover strategies, more effective policies.
4. **For each Bad Thing, what can be done to Contain?** Offsite Backups, documented recovery procedures.
5. **How would you prioritize when Bad Things happen to multiple parts of the business?** If three aspects of your company are impacted, do you need to set priorities so resources are aimed appropriately?

Not sure how to prioritize? Consider for each Bad Thing and you're close to defining your risk. It's:

Risk = BCOD (previous section) × likelihood.

I usually find that companies have a higher risk than they realized. I also usually find that companies have a lot of (relatively) low cost prevention and containment options. These are low hanging fruit. Implement them. Now.

One of the more popular companies in this field, Datto, has a great (and free) Recovery Time Calculator. You can access this by going to http://tools.datto.com/rto/ and entering some of the numbers discussed above.

Business Continuity Solution Strategies

I've really tried to steer clear of talking specific technologies for this book. It really isn't the focus of this book, but I think in this case we need to make an exception. Here are some Business Continuity strategies and solutions, plus some wild card topics you need to consider beyond the traditional localized disaster.

- Equipment failover
- Service (ISP) failover
- BDR based local virtualization
- Cloud based backups/virtualization
- Mobile users
- Cloud services
- Specialized people
- Communication

Let's talk about each of these things:

- **Equipment failover.** When Mr. Scott sabotages the *USS Excelsior* in "*Star Trek III: The Search for Spock's Luggage*," he apparently does so by removing five large ball bearings. Those are apparently critical ball bearings. Knowing what equipment is critical and having a "spare" to either automatically kick in (failover) or have to be manually replaced (some down time, but better than ordering it and waiting for delivery) is a good strategy.

- **Service (ISP) failover.** Thankfully, your Internet provider is rock solid, all the time. Right? Okay, not so much. And this is becoming more critical as we deploy more services through the cloud and rely on collaboration with vendors and customers through the web. So . . . why not have two Internet connections? The second one can be significantly slower. And most UTM's (which connect your business to the Internet) can be configured to handle both ISP connections and automatically use the fastest one available.

- **BDR-based local virtualization.** So, your server is toast. Gone. Buh-bye. If you're backing up your servers to a device called a BDR (Backup Data Recovery), you can "spin up" that server virtually using the last backup stored on the BDR. Your users would then be able to log onto the "server," which would look and act exactly like the server (except a bit slower). You'd have to arrange for the data entered since the last backup to be reentered. But you don't have to be completely down until the server is fixed. Spinning up the server should take less than half an hour. So if you run backups every two hours during the day, you run the risk of "only" losing up to two hours of data.

- **Cloud-based backups/virtualization.** This is similar to the BDR scenario, except in the cloud. Many cloud backup providers include the ability of running your servers in the cloud. There are some drawbacks (the connection speed would be significantly slower than if the server was on premise), but this is a great option if your disaster involved loss of a majority of your site (not only the servers, but your BDR was impacted, as well).

- **Mobile users.** Remote users are dependent on two things: their phones and their laptops and/or tablets. In both cases, the products are relative commodities, but the data (and sometimes software) on them is priceless. Use technologies (i.e., filesharing) that automatically back up documents and data to the cloud, and make sure those choices are centrally managed. Don't rely on your travelling salesperson to remember to copy stuff to his thumb drive. Really. Don't do this.

- **Cloud services.** This is dependent on the specific service. As with backups, services such as Azure and AWS offer differing levels of backup solutions.

- **Specialized people.** Whether the skills be IT-related or not, cross-training and documentation are your best defense against losing a critical person at a critical time.

- **Communication.** *It is almost always the cover-up rather than the event that causes trouble. – Howard Baker.* If something happens, own it. If there's a problem, admit it.

Have You Tested Your Solutions?

There are a number of ways you can test your business continuity solutions. You can do it conceptually (what's called a tabletop method). This is where the parties get together and you simply walk through the process logically.

On the technical side, testing the equipment (and processes) you'll be depending on is critical. Backups need to be tested. So does equipment designated for failover and virtualizations.

Summary:

Here are a few steps you should take at a minimum:

- **Identify key functions and hourly downtime costs.** Work with the rest of your management team on this one. The costs don't need to be spot on accurate.
- **Implement (if you don't have one) a BDR-based BC strategy.** If all you do is back up your servers locally (and to the cloud) using a BDR, this is aces better than without. You'll be able to relatively quickly and painlessly get your servers up and running with a minimum of effort and data loss.
- **Perform a table top disaster review with your management team.** Bring in some pizza and your IT resource. Go over what things could fail and how you would all cope. Identify small things you can do to minimize the risk. Take notes.
- **Business Continuity is affordable.** The cost difference between the technology that just backs up your data and the technology that keeps you operational in the event of significant outages isn't huge. But the difference between being operational and shut down is.

18. CYBER SECURITY – PART I: THE BAD GUYS

What CEOs Need to Know about Keeping Their IT Safe

Why Does Cyber Security Matter to the Small-to-Medium Business?

Boy, I struggled with this topic. It's right up there with Backups and Business Continuity in terms of importance. But the challenge is that the more specific I get, the deeper into technology this goes (which I'm really trying to avoid). Plus, I'll be obsolete before I finish writing.

But let's start with a very specific statement. You don't know enough about cyber security to protect your company by yourself, and you won't when you're done reading this book.

Like every other chapter, the goal here is to educate you enough so you appreciate the seriousness of the topic and how critical it is for you to allocate the appropriate resources to deal with it. You need to engage a resource to work with you to create a true Cyber Security strategy, and help implement, manage, and maintain it. Like . . . repeat after me . . . Simplex-IT (hey, that even rhymes!).

Here's the real struggle you need to understand. The bad guys have figured out how to make money through attacks on companies *of all sizes*. How? Through the exact same tools we've been talking about. Automation. Cloud. Services. Mobile. Every technology that can be used for gathering or accessing data, creating value for a user, learning about your customer, sharing data between devices, etc., can also be used for evil purposes. Technology is morally neutral, unfortunately.

Every second, there are about eight new Internet users added. Every day. And 30,000 new infected websites, *every day*, having some component that can be harmful to end users that go there. Finally there are about 750,000 new unique pieces of malware created daily.[11]

We're used to hearing about the big security breaches. Equifax was the big one in the news when I started writing this section, with as many as 143 million Americans affected. That's almost half of the adult population in the USA. While I'm going through later edits, Uber was in a similarly dubious spotlight. During my final edit, it's Intel and AMD admitting to their processors having security flaws in the news.[12]

The press loves to focus on big security breaches. Let's face it, they're more fun, and we can focus on our outrage and feeling like a helpless victim. There are focused breaches where bad guys use resources specifically aimed at site a they've identified as a worthwhile target. The extramarital site Ashley Madison. Equifax. The Democratic National Committee (during the 2016 Presidential Campaign). They identified the target because they wanted the goods, whether it be customer information, credit card info, or compromising data.

In the case of Ashley Madison (2015), the hackers attempted to blackmail the website owners, threatening to release the user account info if a fee wasn't paid. The owners refused, and the hackers made good on their threat, ruining many careers, reputations, and probably weekend plans.

In the case of Equifax (2017), there was a vulnerability in a piece of software that wasn't properly patched. Exploiting that vulnerability gave the hackers the ability to perform identity theft on a grand scale.

---

[11] According to Sophos

[12] http://www.simplex-it.com/2018/01/meltdown-spectre-patch-not/

And you can draw whatever conclusion you like from the DNC hack.

But back to the smaller-to-medium business world. Back in the day (prior to 2012), the viruses were what was really annoying. These were the viruses that replicated between computers and created havoc to the SMB world, often by destroying data on computers. But the bad guys didn't get any money for it. They weren't profitable, which meant that the people who were creating these "tools" were just being jerks. Their goal was to see if they could do it. Their goal was to vandalize just because they happened to be technically skilled and could. Cyber security was relatively in its infancy, with many companies (large and small) giving it lip service at best. The only parties that made money from these activities were the anti-virus companies and the consultants who were paid to clean up afterwards.

Then ransomware started surfacing. Instead of destroying your data, the aim was to encrypt it, and only they had the key to decrypt the data. The attacker would then charge you a fee or ransom if you wanted to recover that data safely. They accomplished this by developing a program and getting it to run on your network. This was done by either tricking an unsuspecting user to run it for them (from visiting a malware infected website or email), or forcing their way onto the network by taking advantage of holes in the network protection. The program would reach out to the bad guys' mothership and get an encryption key. Then it would go to town and encrypt every document it could get its hands on, using very effective encryption tools. The FBI has said if you've got it encrypted, pay the ransomware costs because you can't go around them (with some exceptions).

If we look at it from the standpoint of a business model, it's a solid model. Quality product (ransomware). Great marketing and product distribution (very thin, with little cost). Reasonably priced (you might not think so if you're so affected). If it weren't for the whole illegal and immoral thing, we'd probably be looking to invest in the technology. And most of these companies are located in countries that absolutely love what these guys are doing. They don't have to be concerned about the law coming after them. So now we don't have to just worry about hackers.

Now we need to worry about entrepreneurs.

That's what's happened in the three or four years since ransomware came. So now these people are highly incentivized to go after your organization.

Malware is Big Business

According to the FBI's Internet Crime Complaint Center (IC3)[13], 2016 saw 298,728 complaints with losses in the area of $1.45 billion. Yup, billion. And although the number of complaints has remained relatively steady since 2012, the financial losses have almost tripled (in 2012, the amount was $525 million). Remember, this is only counting people who have *reported* the activity (and only incidents in the US).

That cool technology that automatically backs up your data to the cloud so you don't lose anything? How different is that from a slightly different tool that copies your data to a third party? The technology that helps you find potential customers to communicate with? How different is that from technology that helps a bad actor exploit his or her next victim?

---

[13] FBI's 2016 Internet Crime Report: https://pdf.ic3.gov/2016_IC3Report.pdf

The challenge is, the bad guys are greedy. They are financially incentivized to find new ways to get money from the good guys (us). And since they've got the money, they're willing to invest big bucks to make it happen.

Yup, we're talking about evil entrepreneurs. But instead of hiding out in secret underground bases with henchmen, cackling evil laughs and snappy repartee with the latest James Bond "No, Mr. Bond! I expect you to access a Flash enabled website without properly patching Flash on your desktop, allowing an attack on your workstation to take advantage of the vulnerability, get past your unsuspecting firewall, get an encryption key and convert all your critical documents into encrypted mush. . .if you don't pay me . . . **Five . . . Hundred . . . Dollars!**"

Yeah, I know. The laser scene in *GoldFinger* was cooler.

Here's part of the challenge. A lot of the bad guys live in countries where this sort of thing isn't only legal, it's a vital part of their economy. So not only can they operate in the open (relatively speaking), they can actively hire (and pay) the best and the brightest folks to be bad guys with an offer of a regular job.

And what have they done? They've created some great, quality products (okay, they're evil products, but still . . . high quality). They've done a great job of "marketing" (as in getting their "customers" to consume their products). And they've (mostly) priced their products reasonably. So most "customers" can afford to pay it.

This is a tough concept to get your head around, but it's important.

Today's hackers have more in common with businessmen and entrepreneurs than ever before. ***And that's what makes them so dangerous.***

So here's what I'm going to do. I'm going to focus on explaining the threat and defining some of the risks. You absolutely won't walk away from here with a magic pill for your security needs. *Because there isn't any.* Cyber Security is a layered strategy. It's a combination of technologies, processes, strategies, and practices.

My goal is to convince you that this is important. It's worth your time. Your energy. And yes, your money. Because it's your organization.

Breaking It Down

Here's the approach we're going to take. Cyber Security is a crime, right? And when we watch TV crime dramas, what are the three aspects of a crime always being brought up? Motive, Opportunity, and Means (you can play the "Law and Order" sound track in your mind right now, if you want. I'll wait).

Motive:	What was the reason the bad guy committed the crime?
Opportunity:	What was the chance provided to the bad guy to commit the crime?
Means:	The bad guy has the ability to commit the crime.

Motive:

This is a book about business, so we're going to keep the topic focused there. But if you imagine any motive for any crime, there's a place for that in Cyber Crime. Personal motives, crimes of passion, just being a jerk. But for our purposes we're going to limit it to:

- $ (through ransom)
- $ (through trickery)

- $ (through blackmail)
- Credentials
- Identity Theft
- Critical Business Information
- Online Reputation
- Access to Resources
- Inflict Damage

Notice that in some cases, the victim might not even realize that they've been successfully attacked. Sometimes precious information can be copied (think financial, customer info, credentials). Other times the computer is used to perform tasks in the background under the control of the bad guys. Or recording keystrokes, or even taking control of the video camera on your laptop. During all of this, the victim is unaware of any of these activities.

Opportunity:

In order for the bad guys to win, they need to have some level of interaction with you (or your technologies). This means that you either "go to them," or they need to "come to you." Some examples:

- Visiting infected websites
- Opening, responding, or clicking links in dangerous emails.
- Social media (sharing information with an app or contact that's a bad guy)
- Using infected media (like a thumb drive)
- Installing applications provided by bad actors (especially on mobile devices)

- Social engineering (someone smooth talks an employee into assisting bad guys)
- Bad guys finding a way into your IT resources
- Bad guys impersonating others online or through email
- Stealing your equipment

Take a minute to look at this list. A big benefit of IT to companies is the ability to connect your resources (whether it be your phone, laptop, server or anything else) to other resources and transfer data between them. The bad guys are creative, and they're incentivized. However you connect to resources, they're out there inventing ways to take advantage of that. And they're pretty good at it.

Means:

If you remember back in the beginning, we defined the term "Exploit." It's a vulnerability in a system which can be exploited by the bad guys. The vulnerability could be found in any component or device that has access to your IT resources. Most malware takes advantage of at least one exploit.

There are five popular ways to introduce the malware to the unsuspecting public.

1. **Infected website.** The user is directed to a website that will apply the malware to the user. The website could be set up by the bad guys, or it was hacked and the malware was introduced. Either way, the malware tries to attack the user's computer.

2. **Email links and attachments**. We've all seen emails that somehow try to get us to open links and attachments, which contain and deliver the malware.

3. **Brute force.** Bad guys find openings in your network or individual computers and try a variety of methods to force their way in.

4. **Eavesdropping.** Sometimes the bad guys just want to "listen" to the Internet traffic from your computer (what websites you go to, your account names, passwords, etc.).

5. **Phishing.** Deceiving users (often through email) into sharing sensitive data with the bad guys.

Next, let's chat about the numerous components that bad guys can try to exploit to interfere with your systems and your data. This is so you can appreciate all the possible ways bad guys can try to "get in."

Go sit down in a coffee shop and do some business on the web. C'mon, you deserve the Grande café Jalapeno banana nutmeg maple bacon lemon with a hint of broccoli (sorry, not a coffee drinker).

When you "go to" a website (or VPN into a site or use email), there are many (dozens, actually) technology components (which can be a device, program, or service) that are working together. Let's take a brief overview (in approximate but really simplified order):

1. Your log onto your computer, and . . .
2. Connect to the coffee shop's wireless network;
3. Which uses the coffee shop's network to connect you to the Internet.

4. On your computer, you open up a browser and connect to your site.

5. DNS is used to identify the location of the website you're trying to access.

6. Your traffic is routed to that location.

7. A server on their site takes your connection request and composes a response.

8. That response is sent back to your computer (mostly reversing the process).

9. You see the website (or whatever the resource is) on your computer.

10. Information is sent back and forth between your computer and the remote site as you take care of business.

Every step listed above (by the way, this is a simplified process) involves a different type of technology, with several different owners and vendors. Steps 1, 2, and 9 are your computer (or mobile device). Steps 3 and 4 are the coffee shop. Steps 5 and 6 are (probably) the Internet Service Provider (or "ISP") for the coffee shop. And 7 and 8 are in the hands of the vendor who has the remote resource that you're interested in (and they possibly have several layers of technology and vendors on their side you don't see).

As each step uses technology components specifically created to interact with other components, each component also has potential exploits that can be used by bad actors to gain access to some level of this process.

This, unfortunately, makes sense. Every component that's been created to aid in communication between devices carries a risk. A wall with a door is more vulnerable than a wall without.

A door that's easy to open and welcoming to strangers is more vulnerable than a door that's meant to protect.

And here's the rub. We want technology to be effortlessly accessible to people who should have access, and equally *in*accessible to those who should not.

Remember, for the first 20 years of the "PC revolution," the goal was to make it easier to connect between devices, locations, and applications. Security wasn't a primary part of the equation. It really wasn't until 2002 that Microsoft, under Bill Gates, started the "Trustworthy Computing" initiative[14], making security a priority.

Let's also be clear. Making components more secure increases the complexity and the cost of the process. Which makes sense. Let's take a simple doorway. How do we make it more secure, and what's the downside?

1. **Simple doorway.** Fast, efficient, cheap. Nothing to open or close. No meaningful limitations. Zero security.
2. **Simple door (doorknob, no lock).** Okay, protecting a bit against the elements. Most anyone can open and close it with little to no training. A bit of security, but not really. But now to get through the doorway, someone needs to turn the knob and push/pull.
3. **Locked door (key).** Okay, now we're adding security. We're limiting the people who can get through the doorway by adding a level of security that we only share with people we want to get through. We use at least one of three types of keys. Better yet, a combination which is

---

[14] For a vendor-neutral description, check out: https://en.wikipedia.org/wiki/Trustworthy_computing

also known as multi-factor authentication . . . more on that later). They types of key are:

a. **Key.** Just that, a physical object that has the ability to open the lock.

b. **Password.** A code that will open the lock when entered through keypad or similar manner.

c. **Attribute.** Retinal scan, facial recognition, fingerprint.

The lock example is deceptively simple. If you've ever shopped at a hardware store for a lock for a door, you know that there are dozens of devices with a wide range of costs. You could also place a living guard (or many) at the door to provide real time monitoring of the door (although that would still be technically a "lock" to the door, limiting access).

To a certain point, all technology components depend on some layer of the above strategy. Part of the challenge is that the cost and complexity increase along with the level of offered security.

All technology components that allow interaction have vulnerabilities. Low cost versions of these components often have serious security risks. More secure versions often include the additional security with either higher cost or slower performance. And they often need to be configured for the appropriate level of security.

Now, let's return to the coffee shop owner and the component she provides in the above example. She wants customers to be happy. She doesn't want them to have to go through hoops and passwords to use what many consider to be a critical service that she provides. The last thing she wants her employees to do is troubleshoot pesky wireless connections. She wants to make accessing the wireless network as simple as possible. And she doesn't have a big budget to purchase and configure equipment with a high level of security that can be more seamless to the customer. All this leads to using minimal security to access her wireless network. The open doorway.

The good news? Everybody can access her wireless network. The bad news? The open doorway allows bad actors to take advantage of that, leaving her customers vulnerable.

Now repeat that assessment for every component that's used to perform the task we described. Every. Single. Component. Has. Potential. Vulnerabilities. Period.

We'll talk about what to do about that in the next chapter.

Summary:

Here are the key takeaways from this chapter:

- The Bad Guys are now financially incentivized.
- The Bad Guys are extremely clever.
- The Bad Guys are constantly looking for new ways to exploit technology that your business uses.
- The Bad Guys can automate this process enough to make the smallest business a reasonable target.

19. CYBER SECURITY – PART II: THE GOOD GUYS

Okay, hopefully, I've succeeded in a couple of things. First, you understand that being a small company doesn't protect or hide you. Second, you get the idea that the bad guys are incentivized, just like any entrepreneur. That means they're eager to find new opportunities to generate value and revenue . . . from you.

Scary, right? Well, it should be . . . if you're not doing anything about it. If your strategy has been unchanged from 2000 when anti-virus software and occasional backups were your solution to everything, you're running on borrowed time—or worse, you've already been hacked and don't even know it.

But let's work on some strategies to reasonably protect your organization.

Bring Somebody In

As I've mentioned throughout this book, I'm not trying to make you an expert in IT. I'm also not trying to "sell" you a specific solution to this complicated problem, especially since the solution would be obsolete the instant the book was published.

What I am trying to do is to give you enough information to help you make informed decisions and have informed conversations with the "experts" that you bring in to help you with your organization.

Depending on the size and complexity of your organization, you may not need to bring in an organization that specializes only in Cyber Security (although you should certainly consider it if your needs are high). But you should make sure that your IT resource is reasonably up to date on their skill sets and solutions and ask them what they do to keep current.

The Compliance Game

In some cases, security requirements are dictated to you by the nature of your industry.

- **HIPAA.** (Healthcare Insurance Portability and Accountability Act). Aimed directly at the healthcare world.
- **SOX.** (Sarbanes-Oxley Act). Primarily aimed at financial disclosures from corporations protecting against accounting fraud.
- **PCI.** (Payment Card Industry). Aimed at organizations that collect payments through credit cards.

We're not going to go into those categories; (Books abound about them.) But it's important for you to know that if your company is regulated by any of these, take them seriously. The penalties for non-compliance are pretty stiff, and ignorance is not a defense.

It's a % Game at Best

Let's set some expectations. Most businesses are increasing their need for remote connectivity and communications. This is true for employees who are working at various remote locations, as well as vendors, customers, and other stakeholders. There is tremendous value in sharing information on a timely and effective basis.

Every time we increase the level of connectivity, we increase the possibility that we can be compromised. That makes sense, when you think about it. The more ways we want to interact, the more technologies we're using and the more components are involved. Each represent a potential spot for the bad guys to identify and use an exploit.

All you can do is manage and minimize the risk. There's no way that you can reduce the risk to zero. At some point, the costs to minimizing the risks outweigh the risk itself.

Always keep that in mind.

Backups

I just want to restate that at the end of the day, a *secure and tested* backup strategy is your last line of defense when it comes to protection against data loss. By that, I mean *all* your important data, which includes data on all systems that remote employees are using.

To repeat . . . untested backups aren't backups. They're promises. I would estimate that 20% of the companies we've reviewed for possible services have had problems with their backups, from not working at all to not backing up everything. In many cases, management was unaware of the problem.

Mind your backups, boys and girls.

Layers

Not too long ago, security was a simple thing. Passwords. Then it was passwords and anti-virus software. Then we added firewalls. Then we added . . . and so it went on. Again, I'm not going to get technical. But let's walk through the layers of potential security from opening up a simple email sent by a bad actor:

1. The user (hopefully) catches that this is a bad request and ignores the email.
2. If not (he clicked the link), web filtering software (hopefully) catches the original link to a known malware site and blocks it.

3. If not, the UTM (router/firewall) runs the site remotely (sandboxing) and determines it's a bad site and blocks it.

4. If not, if there's a file involved (simplified), anti-virus checks the files for known malware payloads and (hopefully) blocks it.

5. If there's a bad web-based component taking advantage of a third party (i.e., java, flash) vulnerability, the component (java, flash) has been updated (hopefully) to block it.

6. If there's a Windows desktop vulnerability at play, the desktop has been patched (hopefully) to close the vulnerability.

7. If not, Anti-Exploit software (hopefully) catches the behavior of the workstation and blocks it, alerting IT.

Each of these steps (if properly implemented) blocks a percentage of the threats. The odds of a threat getting through one of these? Pretty good, unfortunately. Getting through all of them? Pretty slim—*if* they're all implemented, maintained, and monitored properly.

Cyber Insurance

Yup, we're talking old-fashioned insurance, but aimed specifically at your IT side of things. Policies are now available (and at pretty reasonable costs) that provide coverage for exposure of PII or PHI (Personally Identifiable/Health Information), PR expenses, forensic expenses and more. Be careful when you're talking to insurance agents offering these policies, and make sure to include your IT Cyber Security resource in the conversation.

Introducing Behavior and Containment!

Around 2014 or so, I was at a conference put on by Sophos (again, we're a partner of theirs). To be honest, I was seriously considering moving to a different provider (they simply didn't "get" the needs of Managed Service Providers like my organization).

But I was blown away by their strategy for the future of their security products, named "Copernicus.[15]" There were two components. The first was one of complete integration, meaning all of the security pieces monitoring each other (so the anti-virus is monitored by the firewall device, which is monitored by the central portal, and so on).

The second was the recognition that prevention as a be-all-and-end-all strategy, was doomed to failure. The bad guys were getting too good, too resourceful.

So the strategy was modified to include the concept of "behavior" and "containment."

"Behavior" is the concept of security software that would monitor what the computer device is doing. If it would start doing something unusual (such as encrypting files, a common trait of ransomware), the security software would stop that "behavior." In a case such as this, the specific malware would not have to be discovered—just the result of its successful implementation.

Three years later, I can tell you that I like the progress they've made (other vendors have since undertaken similar strategies).

---

[15] https://news.sophos.com/en-us/2015/08/17/join-the-sophos-firewall-revolution-project-copernicus-beta-now-available/ keep in mind that this is over 2 years old, and much has already been implemented.

The 4 Pillars of Cyber Security

Now we get to the meat of the matter. I originally stumbled onto the 4 Pillars concept at a CompTIA presentation on Cyber Security back in 2013. I haven't been able to find the original notes on the presentation, so my apologies on that. But here's how I break down Cyber Security from a management perspective.

- **Product.** This is the best known of the pillars. Companies purchase devices like firewalls, programs like anti-virus and encryption.
- **People.** This is the least known. People are as important as ever. The best most effective lock on a door is useless if an untrained employee keeps propping the door open. Training *all* employees on security best practices and renewing that training on at least an annual basis is more critical today than ever.
- **Process.** Cyber security is a fast changing and evolving world. The bad guys are constantly looking for (and finding) new vulnerabilities to exploit. Those vulnerabilities are then fixed ("patched") by the good guys, who deploy it to their customers. Or we inform our employees about new tricks that the bad guys are using to fool us. But the process has to be in place, and Cyber Security has to be expected to change and evolve.
- **Policy.** Cyber security is a corporate-wide issue. Yet, studies have shown that it's primarily IT and Executive Management that's involved. That's extremely short-sighted. You need to get everybody within the organization involved. Buy-in is critical. You have to effectively communicate the

policies to all employees and define penalties for not following them.

I want to stress here, this is not a book on the details of Cyber Security. I'd be doing you a big disservice if I pretended otherwise. This is one topic where you need to talk to an IT firm that has some level of expertise in security . . . um . . . like Simplex-IT. That said, here are some bullet points that I think should be reviewed with your IT resource. And if the answers are "no" for many of these . . . well, drop me a line.[16]

- Do you have a UTM (Unified Threat Management) device (formerly known as a firewall) at each location?
- Is the UTM:
  o Patched up to date?
  o Enabled with security services? (Modern firewalls include a wide array of security tools and monitoring functionality.)
  o Locked down to minimum access?
- Is an advanced anti-virus installed on all endpoint devices (not the free stuff!)?
- Have you reviewed and implemented security expectations for mobile devices? Remote wipe, encrypted data, etc.?
- Are you aware of how data is being accessed from remote resources, including customers, vendors, and employees?
- For any applications or services that are cloud-based, have you reviewed the security that the cloud provider provides?

---

[16] Seriously, drop me an email at Bobsbook@simplex-it.com

- Is Identity Management properly tracked?
- Do you have any compliance requirements?
- Is security routinely monitored and managed from a top level?
- Is there a method to collect information, such as security logs, network issues, application activity, etc.?
- Have you created an expectation of security knowledge/awareness for your general workforce?
- How are you measuring that level of security knowledge/awareness?
- Do you have specific Cyber Security training in place for the general workforce?
- What Cyber Security skills are needed by internal IT staff?
- What is the expectation for Cyber Security skills for your internal IT staff?
- Is there a defined process to train internal IT staff on Cyber Security?
- If a third party is used to manage security, what credentials and practices do they have?
- If a third party is used, how do you evaluate their compliance with their services?
- Have you created a process for cyber risk assessment?
- For new technology, how is security assessed?
- Do you have any costs defined for security breaches (similar to the exercises we did for backups)?
- Is there a plan in place to deal with a security breach?
- What is your business continuity/disaster recovery plan?
- Have you conducted any kind of security assessment? Have you identified potential problem areas?

- Who amongst your organization should be involved in deciding security policy?
- Is there a formal Cyber Security policy?
- How is the Cyber Security policy communicated to the general workforce?
- Is the general workforce ever tested (simulated phishing attacks) on Cyber Security?
- Is your Cyber Security paid more than lip service by the general workforce?
- Are there penalties for non-compliance?
- Is management held to at least the same level of responsibility for Cyber Security as the general workforce?
- Are answers to the following questions reasonably well defined for your workforce?
  - o What corporate resources (email, data, applications, services) can an employee access using their own personal computer?
  - o What personal business can an employee perform on a company-owned computer?
  - o Are there restrictions to the networks an employee can connect to when conducting sensitive company business?
  - o Are there any restrictions to an employee who wishes to perform business on their mobile device?

Some of these questions are a bit on the technical side. Sorry for that. But they're important for you to discuss with your IT service provider.

It. Doesn't. End. Ever.

Unfortunately, Cyber Security as a significant issue (and cost) is only going to get more complicated. Again, the bad guys are financially incentivized to find new ways to exploit technology. And as new vendors come to market with new ways for us to positively utilize IT, the bad guys are going to find ways to take advantage of it.

Summary:

- Bad guys only have to find one vulnerability in your Cyber Security Strategy. Your Cyber Security strategy has to protect or remove all easily discovered vulnerabilities.
- If your Cyber Security devices aren't configured properly or monitored and actively managed, you lose half the protection (or more).
- Cyber Security needs to be kept up to date.
- Patch Windows. Now. Keep them up to date.
- Patch other tools (Java, Flash, etc.). Now. Keep them up to date.
- Train Employees.
- Don't forget Cyber Insurance.
- Work with an IT firm that brings the appropriate Cyber Security experience. I'm thinking Simplex-IT, of course . . . but that's just how I roll.
- It. Doesn't. End. Ever.

20. PEOPLE

"I love Mankind. It's People I can't stand." - Linus Van Pelt

At the end of the day, people can make or break your organization. On behalf of all IT folks, we've tried to automate as much as possible. But you're still left with . . . people. Whether we're talking security, productivity, customer retention, operations, marketing, product support, development, or shop floor productivity . . . people are going to interact with your IT resources. Forget the warm and fuzzies about employee satisfaction; you need to create an environment where employees are given full freedom and resources necessary to do their job properly (and no more). And that environment needs to be properly communicated to the employees, *with the opportunity for feedback.*

Keep in mind, IT changes. Incredibly quickly. This means that your organization has to adapt to the new realities that IT provides. All the security services, systems, and devices in the world can't protect you effectively when an employee blatantly does things that open your organization up to compromise. Similarly, untrained employees often don't take advantage of the tools provided *because they don't know how.*

Let's talk about the big four:

1. Policies and Procedures
2. Training
3. Onboarding
4. Turnover

Policies and Procedures

Nothing makes for more exciting reading than a Policy and Procedures (PnP) manual. It's right up there with reading Microsoft Licensing Agreements. Chances are that even though your organization is in the small-to-medium size, you've got some type of PnP manual.

The odds are (at least based on my experience) that there's little or nothing about IT in your manual. The usual exception (and it's a good one) is stating that "IT equipment can only be used for XYZ corporation business." That's great. It's a start. Not enough, but it's a start. But here are some items that should be defined to some degree in a good PnP manual:

- **Employee Termination**. What steps need to be taken when an employee leaves (voluntarily or not)?
- **Sanction Policy**. How can employees screw up, and what happens when they do?
- **Computer Use.** What can an employee use company-owned equipment for (outside of work purposes)?
- **BYOD (Bring Your Own Device)**. If an employee owns their own IT equipment, can they use it for work purposes? (We'll talk about this one later.)

Not only should there be some level of documentation (and these are only what I would consider the critical topics), but there should be a regular review of these.

IT Training

Well-trained employees are more effective, motivated, and just better. Hopefully, that's understood. There's no question that using IT resources can be relatively complicated, but the benefit can be significant. Using mail merge in Microsoft Word to write the same letter personalized to 100 people in about the same time it takes to do a single letter? That's enhancing productivity.

Similarly, if an employee has been shown what to look for in a suspicious email, it's less likely they'll fall for a phishing attack. Make no mistake, some of the bad guys *will get through your product-based defenses*, and you'll be dependent on your employee to make judgement.

One of the challenges is that training is often assumed to be an expensive endeavor, both in terms of money and time. That can be true, but it doesn't necessarily have to be.

Let's break down the types of training by skill requirement:

1. **Cyber Security.** The most important, and often the most neglected. As we've discussed, the bad guys are getting more and more creative every day, and often rely on unwitting participation on the part of your employees.

2. **Office Automation**. The most common need. The flagship product, of course, is Microsoft Office. But whatever the tool, train employees to use the product most effectively and efficiently.

3. **Business Intelligence**. There are a lot of tools available where trained folks can generate tremendous value using data from your applications. And these tools are getting easier and easier to use. There's gold in them there databases, people. Go get it!

4. **Line of Business Applications**. Applications that drive your business. This is specialized training and usually the most expensive. But this can be critical, both in terms of normal operations and improving productivity.

5. **IT Technical Training**. If you've got an internal IT department, they need to improve. You need to make sure that they're learning new stuff and that the new stuff is *pertinent to your organization*. If your organization isn't heading in the direction to take advantage of 3-D printing, then it should be considered a hobby for your IT staff.

Old farts like myself often think of IT training solely as sending a person off to a classroom for a day or even a week. And that they'll learn a ton of stuff that's completely useless to your organization, and come back with two hours of useful training.

That ain't the way it is anymore. We've come up with 4 models that SMB's can use to create a learning environment without breaking the bank, and without sending everybody for day-long training sessions that cover 20% of what's needed.

1. Online Training. There are several companies that can create online accounts for employees, giving access to hours of training specifically aimed at not just individual applications (i.e., Word), but specific topics (like using graphics). These resources are usually in the <$25/ month/employee, with the ability to track their utilization and progress.

2. Peer Groups. This informal method takes some time and maybe a champion to get it started, but offer to buy lunch for employees who want to get together once or twice a month and share experiences and tools and tips for specific products.

3. Mini-classes. If you have specific issues that need addressed, find a trainer to come in and run a no-frills focused training session. You don't need day-long classes.
4. Custom training. There are a lot of great training resources, but keep it focused on the areas that benefit your organization.

The Internet has created countless resources for employees to use for training. YouTube alone has created millions of hours of free training content, often focused on one specific topic (as of this writing, Simplex-IT has over 170 videos with over 150,000 views). Most are aimed at product demonstrations and overviews. Go to https://youtube.com/user/SimplexITBob and take a peek.

We also provide a package of videos and exams for our customers to train their employees on Cyber Security (and the tools to track and test them). In about an hour and a half, a new employee can be trained on how to spot phishing attacks, the best practice for passwords, and what makes a good Wi-Fi connection.

We're not the only ones creating and managing this kind of content. Hundreds of sites and resources are available that, with minimal effort and expense, can be used to increase the skill set of your employees.

You must make it a priority. *You* must give them the time and create the incentive for them to do this.

Onboarding New Employees

What do you do for new employees? Yup, there should be cake (we celebrate an employee leaving with a party, but when they start, we slam a ton of paperwork on them).

But from an IT standpoint, is there a standard process that's defined in terms of starting a new employee? I'm not going to cover traditional new employee stuff here, just the IT. Have we defined:

- Standard Accounts. What kind of credentials to systems will they need?
- Equipment. PC, laptop, tablet, phone?
- IT Training. Especially security based, but what do they need to know about IT in your organization?

Why is this important? Because often (especially in smaller organization) there's no specific process. This means that the security access that's given to one employee might be different than the security access given to another employee with the same role. This leads to problems.

Employee Turnover

What do you do for exiting employees regarding IT? This is especially critical if the parting of ways ain't under the friendliest terms.

- Do you have a checklist of what keys, devices, accounts, and passwords each employee has?
- Do you have a procedure to ensure return of materials and changing of credentials?
- Do you have a procedure to ensure email continues to be responded to appropriately?
- Do you have a procedure to quickly handle accounts and passwords if an employee is terminated and you think there's bad blood (or going to be)?

Two special cases to highlight here.

When the person leaving is your primary IT guy (or gal)

The IT person in your organization (if there's only one, or the head of IT) usually has keys to the kingdom. Often it's a *lot* of keys, in terms of passwords and accounts. Several times, we've been brought in to a new customer where the parting with the former vendor or employee hasn't been pleasant. Usually, it works out (however painfully), but there have been a couple of instances where we've had to protect the new customer against possible "revenge" on the part of the former party.

Here's the key thing. As CEO, you should already have all the credentials that are critical to your organization. Whether it be because "you could be hit by a bus" or "it's my equipment," the request is reasonable. The credentials you should have include:

1. Domain registration. Your domain (in my case, "Simplex-IT.com") is my livelihood. I "bought" that domain through a provider (GoDaddy in my case). I need to have access to that account.
2. Licensing. Any software or hardware licensing (i.e., Microsoft, Dell).
3. Social Media. Facebook, Twitter.
4. Cloud backup access.
5. Security software.
6. Local network admin credentials.
7. Cloud services accounts (i.e., Azure, AWS)
8. Local network devices (i.e., switches, router/firewalls, UTM's)

As a vendor providing services, I'm concerned if a CEO asks for these credentials. Not that they shouldn't be given them. But I don't want the CEO either mucking with the configuration or bringing in somebody else to muck with them. So, we have a conversation where we stress that these credentials should only be used in the case of an emergency. And (when possible) we create separate credentials from the ones we use so we can identify if they're used without our knowledge. Bottom line, *we give the credentials.*

If the person leaving is the only IT resource, and it's not a happy parting, you should already have a new IT resource on hand (even if it's temporary) who can quickly make changes to the credentials to guarantee that the soon-to-be former employee can't do something rash. You might also create some level of incentive to encourage that they play nice (depending on the circumstances, this isn't always possible).

Email

Handling the email for a former employee is also tricky. Technically, it's straightforward. It comes down to a few questions. Let's take the case of John Smith is leaving Acme Widgets, and his last day is today:

- Who should have access to all of John Smith's email data (including calendar, contacts, and the like)?
- If someone sends an email to John Smith, who should it go to?
- Should there be an automatic reply to new emails saying John's no longer with the company?

- Should emails sent to John Smith go to John's replacement when that person is on board?
- Should the replacement for John Smith have access to John's historical email, calendar, and contacts when they come on board?

It's best if you can create some company standards to these questions. Of course, there may be some special exceptions (how you handle the CFO leaving might be different from an intern), but standards make exceptions easier to handle.

BYOD

We want people to be productive. We want people to be productive when they need to be. A lot of people own their own IT devices, whether it be tablets, PC's, mobile phones. They may want to use those devices to do their job. This would make them more effective and efficient than they would otherwise be. We like increased productivity, right?

Here's how the question is asked:

"Hey, boss. Can I use my home computer to access company applications over the weekend? That way I'll be able to complete the project on time and not cost you any additional money."

Wow. Your answer is absolutely Yes (and probably with a teary-eyed "You had me at . . .*and not cost you. . .*")!

Same question, phrased a tad differently:

"Hey, boss. Can I use my home computer to access company applications over the weekend? You have no idea whether I've got malware and viruses on it, or whether it's been hacked and people are recording all my keystrokes. But that's okay, if I've got a virus, I'll be sure to share!"

Hopefully, your answer is slightly different. Because it might cost you additional money. A lot, in fact.

The more you allow people to legitimately work at their jobs from various locations, the higher the productivity. However, the risk grows if you can't manage it. How do you know they're going to access a company resource safely, and they're not using a system that's already been compromised and is recording every keystroke so now someone knows how to get into your corporate systems? The chain is only as strong as the weakest link.

Here's a tricky one, and you may have created it yourself. If you've put a policy in place to define what an employee can use their own personal IT devices for at work, you need to be concerned about what data they still have on that device.

At the very least, you should have a policy that exiting employees must sign a document declaring that they've removed all corporate data from their personal devices.

At best, you should be using tools that allow you to remove that data remotely.

Of course, the easiest answer is . . . buy them a tablet, laptop, or phone that they can take home with them.

Keep in mind the reality is if an employee has access to sensitive information and wanted to copy that information for their own purposes (prior to dismissal), it is an expensive undertaking to prevent. This is especially true if you're encouraging productivity by allowing remote access to resources through employee-owned devices. That's why it's important to remove access to these resources at the earliest appropriate opportunity (when you're dismissing employees).

You also have employees who want to access their own personal resources using company devices. Do I want *that*? This gets back to some of the security questions. If we're letting employees use their work computer to shop online or access social media, that raises other concerns. What if an employee is surfing inappropriate websites? Or making comments that reflect poorly on the company? Or committing fraud? You need to create a policy that reasonably defines what a person can (and/or can't) do on their company computer.

Summary:

- Train your people to use IT resources responsibly. Especially on Cyber Security issues.
- Create an onboarding procedure for new employees.
- Create an "offboarding" procedure for employees leaving.
- Review the PnP categories included here and decide what's important for your organization.

21. PLUMBING

"My computer is just too fast. Can we slow it down somehow?"

—Said nobody. Ever.

Plumbing Matters

One of the most frequent complaints about computers is, "It's too slow." And often it becomes a finger-pointing session between the users and the IT resources. It's right up there with, "This chicken tastes funny," and "There's something not right with my car." It tells us there's a problem, but doesn't go far enough to tell us where to look.

But it underlies a critical point. The success of your organization is in part dependent on systems running "fast enough."

Sometimes the challenge of "slow computers" is because the hardware is underpowered. Sometimes the users have unrealistic expectations. As Douglas Adams said in *Hitchhiker's Guide to the Galaxy*, "Time is an illusion. Lunchtime doubly so."

One other area to consider is data flowing between devices, networks, and locations (even between continents). Data flows. Everywhere. Whether it be:

- Your health monitoring device on your wrist sending data to your phone
- Productivity information sent from a machine on a shop floor to a primary server half a world away
- A consumer trying to find where the shoe store is at a mall kiosk (yes, there are still malls . . . I think).
- A database server receiving (or transmitting) application data to hundreds of workstations around the building (or the world)

- An employee looking up customer information on his laptop, while sipping coffee at a café half a world away from his office
- Another employee looking up the same customer information from her desktop right down the hall from your servers

I use the concept of plumbing to communicate this resource. Simply put, how thick is the pipe (in terms of speed) being used to transmit data relative to the need?

It's a question of how fast can we transfer data between systems. Today, most systems inside a network built of an office building are transmitting at approximately one billion digits each year as a binary 1 or 0, 1 billion bits per second, or 1,000 megabits. There are two units of measurement thrown around:

1. Megabit (Mb). This is one million bits (1's or 0's).
2. Gigabit (Gb). This is one billion bits (1's or 0's).

So 1,000Mb = 1Gb. Sometimes you'll hear the term "bytes" instead of "bits." A byte is simply 8 bits (which is how letters and numbers are stored). If someone says we have a "6 Megabyte file," that means they have a 48 Megabit (6*8) file.

Unfortunately, storage and memory (hard drive space and ram) are usually measured in bytes, and transmission speeds are measured in bits per second.

When we're talking about transmitting data, we're really just talking about the transmission rate versus how much we're looking to transmit. Capacity versus consumption. And here are three simple rules to start with:

1. Data flowing within your physical location is usually significantly faster than stuff flowing into the cloud.
2. Data flowing through a wired connection is usually significantly faster than stuff flowing through a wireless component.
3. If you're not monitoring your network traffic, you're probably not getting the most out of it.

Some of the most common problems:

1. You're using your network for your phone system (VOIP) and nobody's paying attention to the network traffic (voice data should be handled very different from other types of data).
2. You've got wireless connections galore.
3. You're housing a web server at your location, bringing people into your network.
4. You're providing remote employees with business resources housed within your physical location.
5. You've got devices using both wired and wireless at the same time.
6. You're not monitoring your network traffic, from a quantity, quality, or security perspective.

Just like the plumbing in your house has a number of different pipes and connections that can get clogged or congested, so too can your internal network. The bigger the "pipe" (using the metaphor of the pipe's diameter), the more data can flow per second. So let's talk about the components of our plumbing.

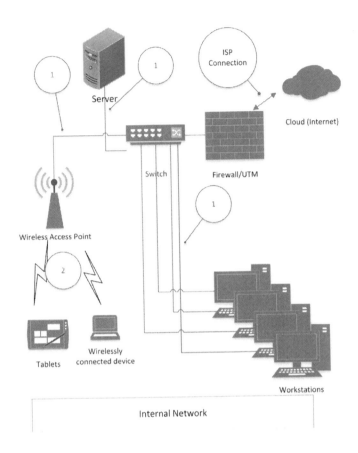

Internal Network

The figure above is a simplified representation of most business networks—the stuff inside your building talking to each other through a combination of wired and wireless connections. Let's walk through the pieces:

1. **Dev(ices).** These are the devices that are sending or receiving data elsewhere using the network. These could be desktops, laptops, mobile devices, printers, security

cameras, shop floor devices. Devices connected by wire (item #1) transmit either 10Mb to 1Gb/second. Devices connected through wireless connections (#2) are transmitting between 50 and 1,000Mb/second (usually *much* closer to the lower number). These are the most common creators of data for most businesses, and include all of your local users.

2. **WAP (Wireless Access Point).** This physical device is what connects all of your wireless devices to your network. Don't go cheap on these devices. First of all, performance isn't a given. Second is security. Wireless devices are a lot easier to hack into (they don't require a physical connection). The speed and security of WAP devices are constantly improving. At the end of the day, however, your WAP devices are supporting the data transmission for all (potentially many) wireless devices connecting to it. It's easy for the WAP to become over-taxed, becoming a bottleneck. And wireless networks are notorious for delivering lower speeds than promised, for a wide variety of technical, environmental, and security reasons. The advertised speed of the WAP (often in the 400-1000Mb/sec range)? That gets cut down (often dramatically) by every additional device that connects to it, every wall and every electronic device between it and the devices connecting to it. Your speed may vary. Greatly.

3. **(Sw)itch.** A switch is a physical device that Devices and WAP's connect to. Usually it can handle 8, 16, 24 or 48 "ports" or connections. Switches can be combined or "stacked" together to handle much larger organizations. They are the glorified "traffic cops" of data traffic (which

includes voice traffic if your organization is using VOIP or Voice Over IP phones). Switches can be configured to prioritize different kinds of traffic, block parts of the network from seeing each other, and assist in trouble-shooting traffic issues. Switches that are capable of helping manage the traffic are called "managed" switches. Ones that aren't capable are called "unmanaged" switches. Usually, switches are capable of handling 1Gb traffic, but older ones are in the 10 or 100Mb range. All devices connected to your network are directly or indirectly connected to a switch (or a device acting like a switch).

4. **Server.** This device (think of it as a huge desktop) is, at the heart of it all, doing what the name implies. It's "serving" the request of other devices. There are many different types of servers: database servers, email servers, application servers, file and print servers, and more. The key thing for this discussion is that servers may be sending and receiving data to and from dozens of devices simultaneously.

5. **UTM (aka, "firewall" and/or "router").** This communication and security device (you'll recall from earlier discussion that UTM stands for "Unified Threat Management" device) handles the communication between your network and another network (usually the entire Internet). In this particular case, the UTM is handling all traffic from all devices going out to the cloud (or anywhere else).

In the case of servers, and UTM's, these devices are sending and receiving data from many devices simultaneously. The data connections (both labelled #3) between the server and the switch should be as robust and have as large a "pipe" as possible.

Any time you're looking at slowdowns, trace the map from the device of the user that is experiencing the slow down to its destination (say a server) and back. Those are the potential culprits (including the devices themselves).

To the Cloud!

Back in the day (warning: Geek nostalgia time) when I was "young," I had a device that used a modem giving me a blinding speed of 300bps. Yup, that's 300 bits, which at 8 bits per byte or character translates to 37½ characters per second. So in one second, I could transmit: "I feel the need . . . the need for speed!!" and really, **really** mean it, and have a half second left for reflection.

Boy, have we changed and improved since then.

First of all, the modem was primarily a one device, one modem, one phone line, one connection kind of thing. Now we have ISP (Internet Service Provider) connections, which offer several different types of technologies for connecting your organization to the Internet. And we've gone through several different technologies: DSL, T-1, cable, fibre, microwave, and satellite, just to name a few.

A couple of things to keep in mind:

1. This stuff changes. If your agreement with your ISP is more than a year old, dust off the agreement and see what's out there. It's not unusual to see new options, whether they're improved speed, reliability, or the like. Don't be afraid to call your ISP and ask whether there are

any new options or upgrades. This is especially true with organizations that are using T1 or DSL technologies.

2. Up and down ain't the same. Often (especially with cable) the upload speed for the Internet is about 25% of the download speed. You may be downloading at 20Mbps, but you're only uploading at 5Mbps.

3. It's slower than internal. Most fiber connections (the new holy grail of high speed Internet) are somewhere around 20Mbs or so at best. That's a far cry from the 1Gbs speed of your internal network.

4. All Internet through one pipe. Most organizations have either one Internet connection or a second, much slower (and cheaper) Internet connection as a fallback or failover option. All devices, including desktops, laptops, phones, servers, that are accessing off-premise resources through the cloud are going through that single pipeline. Which means that traffic congestion is a lot more common in Internet traffic.

But that just gets you to the Cloud, the Internet. Let's say you want to connect to a cloud-based service. That can be anything stored anywhere outside of your network, whether it be a website, cloud service, remote desktop, streaming video, vertical application, or any other service. The traffic goes through your network, through the UTM out to "the cloud" through your ISP. Then it continues through to the host of the service, to the servers providing that service on their site (by way of UTM's and switches on their site). They read your request and send the response back to you (retracing the steps). Your device then presents the response to you (in the form of an email, website, application screen, or that darn cute video of the hamster doing an impersonation of Gene Kelly in *Singing in the Rain*).

If appropriate, that back and forth continues as you reply to emails, select website options, or add pithy comments to the hamster video.

The important thing to note is that most cloud providers have invested a lot more money than you and I have to make sure that their services are capable of handling high numbers of simultaneous connections, both in terms of performance and security.

Remote Plumbing:

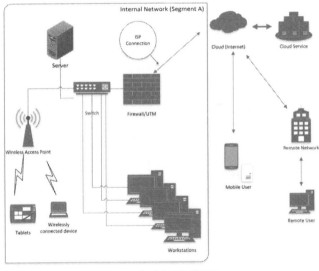

Remote Connection Plumbing

Internet (cloud) traffic is also all about plumbing. Consider the above graphic. Segment A still represents your office. But we're adding 3 common cloud-based connections.

Cloud Services

When users inside your office connect to an internet service (whether it be a web site, services like Office 365 or cloud resources like Microsoft Azure or Amazon Web Services), they all connect through your internet connection provided by your Internet Service Provider (or ISP). Everybody in your office is using that connection, so it's important to have a big enough pipe (bandwidth). The Cloud Provider usually has enough bandwidth on their side.

Remote Users

Users from outside your office often need to connect to services located on your site. This can be employees, customers or vendors. They could be working from home, or a coffee shop, or their own business locations. They could be accessing files, a web site or applications located on your internal network.

For them to connect to your network, plumbing first takes them through the network that they're currently connected to, with the same speed constrictions you face. Then they go through the cloud and then to your resources on your on-premise network.

The reason this is important is that if your remote user is connecting at a coffee shop that doesn't see the need for a high-speed connection, their connection is going to be poor and *there's nothing you can do about it.* The performance for your connection will be no better than the slowest component in the connection chain.

Mobile Devices

For mobile devices, it's a similar diagram, with one exception. The mobile device often connects through the Digital Network provided by the mobile network. All commercials aside, as we all know, connection speed can vary wildly for the strangest reasons.

The temptation, of course, is to connect to any wireless network that would have us. The problem is that free Wi-Fi sites are a great place for the bad guys to hang around and play havoc on unsuspecting users and unprotected mobile devices (which far too many of them are).

Cloud versus On Premise

Bad plumbing equals bad user experience, which is a bad thing. A rule of thumb: The more external resources need to access your internal network resources, the more you should consider migrating those resources to the cloud. Cloud service providers will always be able to provide faster and more reliable internet services than you will.

Monitoring the Plumbing

A large percentage of complaints about IT surround the performance: the systems of performance, of the computer's performance, the network's performance. If you do not know, you don't know how each piece is operating. You don't know what's making things slow or how much memory the systems have. As an industry, we're getting much better at monitoring and measuring specific components of the computer—how much memory the system is using, how much processor speed, disk space (and speed), that sort of thing.

It's when you combine these components and spread them out over a network where we're showing lapses. If you're not monitoring it, you're not measuring it. If you're not measuring it, you're not going to be able to determine what the problem is, let alone the solution.

Somebody needs to be watching the plumbing.

Summary:

- Don't get bogged down in the subtle nuances. 1Gb is 1,000 times faster than 1Mb.
- What's your Internet speed? Find out! Also, find out the last time you checked with your provider for faster or cheaper connectivity.
- Are your switches all Gb (gigabit) or faster?
- Are your switches all managed switches? And are they configured properly?
- Do you have a separate wireless network for employees and guests?

PART III

Now What?

22. BOB'S IT TREND REVIEW

When I started in the wonderful IT world (wrote my first program in 1975 in high school on a Digital Equipment Corporation PDP-8), IT for small-to-medium organizations (let alone individuals) was a pipe dream. If you wanted something typewritten, you used a typewriter, which is essentially the same device in terms of core functionality from its origin in the late 19th century. We stuck with the typewriter until the word processor replaced it for the majority of businesses in the 90's. Since then, new concepts, trends, services, and delivery models have constantly been invented, re-invented, and discovered. Unfortunately, many times the definitions are driven by the primary vendors of the new service (or the vendors of the services threatened by the new stuff).

What we're going to do here is review a lot of the newer concepts and give fairly simple definitions. Fair warning, many of them will be generalizations. Someone concerned about 100% accuracy will probably be cursing my shadow halfway through.

It's not unusual for the new concept to be actually old stuff with a twist.

But there's nothing like a good buzzword or TLA (Three Letter Acronym) that makes an IT geek feel superior. If it's a relatively new or hot new term, we could even be talking about a 10-20% increase in a consultant's hourly rate!

With that, let's dive in!

3D Printing

3D printing is a process where a device (which can be as simple as a reconfigured inkjet printer) is used to take a design created using any of several Computer-Aided-Design (CAD) packages and "print" them by adding material (usually some kind of polymer) one layer onto another. A simple 3D printer can run well under $2,000.

One of the first popular uses of 3D printing was for prototyping samples during the design process. As the technology matures, 3D printing is now used for actual final product, including metal. Another term often used is Additive Manufacturing.

Printed parts are becoming more and more accepted as providers of manufactured products.

Big Data

The term Big Data often seems to be an offshoot of Big Brother, coined by George Orwell in his dystopian novel *1984*. The Hollywood implication is that through Big Data, everything is known about everybody all the time.

Ah, no. Big Data is based on four significant advances in technology, all happening in the past decade:

1. Maturation of data collection tools and techniques. If it happens and a device is involved, data concerning the event can be collected.
2. Deployment of low-cost high-speed Internet connections. The data is collected. Now it can be transmitted cheaply.
3. Storage and processing power continuing to rapidly improve. The size of the data set to be analyzed isn't daunting to today's processors and storage devices.

4. BI (Business Intelligence) tools can now find trends and hidden drivers for behavior patterns. This is especially true when partnered with intelligent human drivers.

Of these advances, #4 is the key element that is truly new and revolutionary. And it's really just beginning. Big Data isn't just something to be applied to the data within your organization. It can also be used by your organization against other data sets. Want to expand to a new market, but can't decide where? Use data from your applications to identify customer traits using a third party's Big Data tools and services. That way you see whether a potential site has those traits. Look before you leap.

<blank> as a Service

It started with "Software as a Service," or SAAS. Then it was "Hardware as a Service" (HAAS). Followed by "Infrastructure as a Service" (IAAS). And there actually is a "Ransomware as a Service" (RAAS, for those who want to be a crook and thief, but don't want to actually do the work). The latest concept is "Security as a Service" (SecAAS). Other terms I've run into are (I'll just use the first word here to save trees): Data, Function, Logging, Mobility, Monitoring, Payments, Platform, and Recovery.

Simply put, it's renting—except instead of renting a home or piece of equipment, you're paying a monthly fee for whatever the heck it is the third party provides. Depending on the offering, either all of the monitoring and maintenance of the offering will be provided through that monthly fee or you'll be given the tools necessary to monitor and manage the offering yourself.

Many cloud services fall under the "Software as a Service" model. You can acquire the cloud services by paying a monthly fee. Services can be stopped, services can be upgraded, services can be changed, services can be cancelled. This usually bypasses capital investment and delegates some (or all) of the managements of the services to that third party. This makes it much easier in terms of budgeting, managing, maintaining, and growing these services. Upgrades are usually (not always) handled by the service provider and included (again, not always) in the monthly fee. And often the services can be easily expanded to accommodate growth within your organization.

"Hardware as a Service," or HAAS, is another common example. This is closer to a traditional rental agreement, commonly used by Managed Service Providers. In a HAAS agreement, the provider would provide actual equipment (UTMs, switches, desktops, printers, pretty much any IT equipment). You'd pay a monthly fee for the equipment. In return, the provider would support the equipment and also include some kind of agreement on when that equipment would be replaced. So paying a monthly fee for a desktop, as an example, would include an automatic replacement of the desktop (with optionally the latest appropriate hardware configuration and operating system software) at no additional charge.

Cloud

Okay, here's the fun part. There is no specific definition of "the cloud." Everyone from the media to vendors have bastardized the definition for the sake of either simplicity or to further their own product launch.

The simplest (and in my opinion best) definition of the cloud is . . . the Internet. Which means the cloud is nothing new. Yet, that's not quite true. The cloud has revolutionized the usability and scalability of resources located on the Internet.

It's where the fun resides. What the cloud has done is introduce an incredible amount of flexibility for how you acquire and maintain the IT resources for your organization. Technically, when you go to *Google* or *Yahoo*, those are servers that are "in the cloud." Now, it gets tricky. With some cloud resources (Amazon's AWS or Microsoft's Azure as examples), you're going to rent traditional IT resources (such as servers). Other examples will involve a cloud-based resource, like Microsoft's Office 365 providing cloud-based email. Other services provide complete business applications (like Salesforce.com). These examples only require an Internet connection. No capital investment for the servers or software. Oh, you will need a credit card. Don't forget that.

Internet of Things

Any device that can have built-in capacity (technology) to help it perform its function can be enhanced to extend its controls or share its data through the Internet. This is manifested in three ways:

1. Control. This allows control of the device remotely. So lights in a building can be turned down when nobody is present. A car can be started in an airport parking lot after landing so it will be warm. A shop floor device can kick off an automated process because it's scheduled to do so.

2. Diagnostics. Metrics can be shared that allow appropriate care and maintenance to be performed. Devices generating too much heat. A failed component.

3. Business Intelligence. Your TV knows what programs you watch. Your phone knows what wireless networks you connect to. Your car knows where you drive and how heavy your foot is on the gas pedal. Your smart watch knows your workout habits. Your video game knows what games you like. Your phone, tablet, laptop, and desktops know what websites you go to. Mall kiosks know what shops people are looking for. Your home security system knows when you're home (or not). All of these are gold mines of data, waiting to be unlocked.

Mobile Device Management

Mobile devices are here to stay. As more and more mobile applications are created for business purposes, so, too, are more and more examples of malware. And the mobile industry (and users, like, um . . . you and me) has been late in developing the appropriate tools and mindset to fully protect these devices.

It's becoming more and more common for people to use their personal mobile devices to access business information.

MDM (Mobile Device Management) is usually offered as a cloud-based service hosted by a third party (Microsoft and Sophos are two examples), which gives you the capability to monitor and manage most (iPhones from Apple and Google's Android) mobile devices. These services give you the ability to support, maintain applications, and monitor the security of the devices. It also gives you the means to remove data and applications, which is great for lost devices and suddenly former employees.

Two decisions you need to make (as previously discussed) are what business actions people can perform on their personal devices, and what personal actions employees can perform on their business-owned devices. Add to that whether you want to monitor (and possibly support) devices owned by employees. If you do, that increases the responsibilities (and costs) for your IT support. If you don't, you don't have any way of knowing if the mobile devices of your employees have somehow been compromised.

Net Neutrality

This isn't a technical issue, but it will probably affect all of us. The Internet has long been a place where Internet Service Providers (ISPs) cannot favor data over another based on user, content, platform, website, service, application, or the like.

ISPs (and some larger content providers) would like this to change. If they could charge content providers extra for "faster" speed, this gives them an additional revenue source. An ISP can make the website or streaming media 25% faster if you go to the "preferred" vendor (who's kicking in the extra $'s for this to happen).

Most in the tech world (outside of ISPs) oppose the idea, saying that it would put startups in a position where it would be very difficult to compete.

In 2015, the Federal Communication Commission (the FCC in the US) officially adopted net neutrality. As of this writing, the FCC is reversing that.

Remote Desktop/Remote Application/Terminal services

Over the years, the term for this has changed, but the idea is the same. A server is configured to allow devices (laptops, desktops, low-cost dumb terminals) to connect from anywhere. Instead of running programs on the connecting devices, the performance of the applications is handled on the server. The display is transmitted to the connecting device (so the user sees the desktop on her display) and interacts with it as they would with a normal desktop screen.

This significantly lowers the hardware and configuration requirements on the connecting device (all it's doing is display, keyboard, and mouse). Remote Desktop and Terminal Server technology show a full desktop environment (including all programs, shortcuts, and documents). Remote Application technology runs only specific applications.

This strategy is great for connecting remote users to applications installed on servers that are on-premise (or in the cloud).

Social Media

There are a lot of books out there about social media and business, and I won't pretend to be an expert on it. However, there are a few things you need to consider:

1. Facebook is for Business->Consumer; LinkedIn is for Business->Business.
2. Hey, old folks (like me)! Remember the big deal about needing an email address? And then the big deal about needing a website? Now, it's social media.
3. Assume that anything you (or anyone else) post on social media is going to be accessible to the general public.
4. Aim your social media presence at your intended marketing target.
5. SEO (Search Engine Optimization), or how high up you rank when folks search for companies like yours,

is a never ending (and not necessarily cheap) process. More companies are implementing paid advertising through programs like Google Ad Words or LinkedIn Campaigns. If you work with these programs, make absolutely sure you create performance metrics so you can define what works and what doesn't.

6. Keep your content fresh.

Virtual Reality/Augmented Reality

Okay, bear with me on this one. Because VR and AR are going to matter to businesses . . . and probably sooner than we realize.

Virtual Reality has been around for some time. I remember being at a conference in the late 90's, wearing a set of goggles and peering over a virtual ledge. The computer was able to monitor my movements and changed the display for me. I walked forward, the display shifted forward. I leaned over and saw what "was" directly beneath me (albeit in an obviously animated "universe"). Pretty simple, pretty limited.

Times change, and so has the technology. The artificial representation of two of the five senses (sight and sound) has become pretty amazing, and close to real time. Goggles for sight and headphones for sound immerse people into whatever the software presents to the user. A third sense, touch, is starting to make its way into the business through techniques like force feedback (which simply adds differing levels of resistance against the actions of the user), and the applications to use this technology are just getting started. Applications where surgeons are able to work without a natural line-of-sight. Military training on learning how to disarm bombs. Prototyping devices prior to any manufacturing.

The entertainment world in terms of games goes without saying, but tourism and concerts are also getting ready to release applications. 2018 is going to see a number of these devices (mostly in the entertainment and gaming world, but that's bound to change).

Lesser understood, but equally interesting, is Augmented Reality (AR). Also known as "Merged" Reality, AR is where a person's view (directly or indirectly) of the physical word is enhanced with artificially-generated sensory input. A simple version of this would be the Pokémon Go mobile application, where the app would apply the image of a "wild Pokémon" over the image of the "real" surrounds of the player (seen by the device's camera).

Thankfully, AR has many more possibilities. Architects are using it to display walk-throughs of their projects (or table-top designs) for their clients. Think of the movie *Minority Report*, where screens and objects are displayed in front of you as part of what you view (so an object is floating on your desk in front of you). Microsoft is pushing their new HoloLens product (coming out in 2018), which is more business-oriented than the general VR devices currently on schedule to be released.

Virtualization

Back in the old days, if you wanted a server, you bought a server. A physical device. Need two servers? Buy two. Need five? Buy five, and so on. Somebody had the brilliant idea, what if we combined these servers into one physical device?

In other words, there's one physical server. It's running (as separate programs) each of these separate servers, sharing the physical resources like memory, hard drives, CPU's, power supplies, peripherals. To users connecting to these servers, there's no difference between a "physical" server and a "virtual" server. But the hardware costs are significant (estimates run between 20 and 40%). You're no longer tied to specific hardware (migrating virtual servers between physical servers is relatively easy), and coming up with Business Continuity plans is made much simpler. Adding additional resources to virtual servers (or workstations, this technology works just as well for them) is relatively simple. Then we can "chain" physical servers together and have them share large collections of hard drives. This means that if a physical server fails, all of the virtual servers running on that physical server would automatically "fail over" to the surviving physical server, with little or no interruption to the end users accessing the virtual servers.

Two companies, Microsoft (with Hyper-V) and VMWare (VMWare) have pretty well cornered the market for the small-medium business world (although there are alternatives).

Cloud-based services, like Microsoft's Azure and Amazon's AWS, and cloud-hosting companies, like Rackspace, use these technologies extensively.

23. STRATEGIES FOR MANAGING IT FOR YOUR ORGANIZATION

We're nearing the end of our journey. I hope I've been able to shed some light on why IT is important from a business perspective and things that you as non-technical management need to understand (without falling off the geek cliff).

Let's now talk about how you want your IT to be implemented, monitored, and supported for your organization. Each method has plusses and minuses. Each has costs and benefits and risks. And let's make this abundantly clear. Each of these strategies can work, and each of them can fail spectacularly. Yeah, I know. Helpful, ain't I?

But you need to decide how IT is going to be supported and enhanced for your organization.

First Strategy: Internal IT Staff

Ah, the old standby. This is where you hire employee(s) who have the skill set and experience necessary to manage your IT resources. When work is needed beyond their capacity or skill set, they arrange for a vendor to come in for the project. Otherwise, the day-to-day operational responsibilities is/was on them.

a. **Benefits:** The primary benefit is one of control. As their employer, you have full control over these human resources. The second benefit is one of focus and understanding. Employees should have a better understanding of the culture, needs, and focuses of your organization than an outsider, but that has to be encouraged (if not required) by you. I've seen many organizations where the internal IT staff has no clue what their own company does "for a living."

b. **Risks:** For smaller organizations, this situation stifles growth on the part of both IT and the IT employees. If you're relying on your IT employees to help the organization grow in terms of using Information Technology, how are your IT people growing themselves? And often internal IT personnel are self-taught. That doesn't mean they've learned best practice methodologies, and documentation is often lacking.

c. **Why should you do this?:** For organizations with extremely unique IT requirements, it's important that your IT resources are managed by someone with the focus and priority to support you appropriately. Also organizations that are extremely focused on control of their IT resources and reluctant to share responsibilities and access to third parties. This same mentality will make it very difficult to take advantage of many cloud resources and services.

d. **Why shouldn't you do this?:** This strategy is usually more expensive than others presented here. It's also difficult (for smaller organizations) to have an efficient IT strategy with an IT workforce that has a wide spread of skills necessary (i.e., cloud, virtualization, desktop, mobile, security, database). Only bringing in vendors for specific projects means that it's a buyer-seller relationship, not a partner relationship, so they're primarily interested in the project only (or worse, setting you up for the next project).

Second Strategy: MSP (Managed Service Provider)

Ah, the latest standby. The term MSP is getting to be as used (and abused) as "cloud," "<blank> as a service," and "e<blank>."

To be clear, my company (Simplex-IT) is a Managed Service Provider. So, yeah . . . I'm part of the problem.

The core belief behind the MSP model is that there is an agreement between your company and the MSP (let's say Simplex-IT . . . I mean, a guy can dream, can't I?). This agreement defines the level of service provided to the customer not based on hours, but results. This agreement can include all levels of service, including Help Desk, Vendor Management, User Management, Performance Management, Security Management, Patch Management, and monitoring of all the devices, applications, and processes we've been discussing. For a fixed monthly fee.

Underneath the MSP model lies an array of tools, services, and best practices that allow the MSP to monitor, manage, maintain, and support organizations with a high degree of automated preventative maintenance, minimizing the need for costly unplanned issues and downtime.

a. **Benefits:** The first benefit is one of cost. Usually, the cost of an MSP agreement is significantly less than the cost of internal IT, if you're comparing apples to apples. MSP's have larger technical staff, so there is a greater pool, variety, and depth of technical skills. You (should) have a much more manageable budget for IT expenses. The MSP should engage you and your staff for creating a path to the future in terms of utilizing IT moving forward and keep you informed of new developments in the industry.

b. **Risks:** Guess what! Not all MSP's are created equal. MSP's have their culture, just like your organization.

A cultural mismatch between your organization and an MSP can be very damaging and frustrating. This is especially annoying if the agreement with the MSP is a long, multi-year one. Also, some MSP's don't share access to their monitoring tools and documentation. Finally, (and this is a big one), the MSP relationship only works if the MSP understands the fundamental requirements of your organization and takes your high-priority issues just as seriously as you do.

c. **Why should you do this?:** For organizations with "standard" IT requirements, why spend the time to build an IT support structure within your organization when you can simply take advantage of one that's already built? A good MSP should already have backup strategies, security strategies, policies and procedures, and mobile device management solutions configured with their best practices. They only need to configure to your specific needs, based on what makes your organization unique. And the cost will be less than implementing or maintaining an internal IT department (unless you implement an internal IT department on the cheap).

d. **Why shouldn't you do this?:** For organizations with extremely unique IT requirements, it's important that your IT resources are managed by someone with the focus and priority to support you appropriately. Also so for organizations that are extremely focused on control of their IT resources and reluctant to share responsibilities and access to third parties. This same mentality will make it very difficult to take advantage of many cloud resources and services.

Third Strategy: CoMITs (Co-Managed IT Services)

Ah, the newest entry. Actually, the CoMITs term is one we invented (the acronym, not the co-managed part). The term is relatively new (I first heard it in 2016), but we here at Simplex-IT have been providing this for about six years. As of writing this book, Simplex-IT is providing CoMITs level service to about 25% of our customers. The bottom line is that CoMITs is a hybrid between Internal IT and an MSP agreement.

The MSP model is dependent on the implementation of monitoring and management tools and services. In the CoMITs model, the internal IT resources are given access to these tools to increase their productivity.

A CoMITs agreement also has a great amount of flexibility. If the internal IT resource is primarily good with desktops, the CoMITs agreement can place the management of the servers and infrastructure devices in the hands of the MSP. If the internal IT can handle most issues, but is lacking with database technology and there's a critical application relying on SQL server, the MSP can take responsibility for managing the performance of that resource.

The core belief behind the CoMITs model is to take the best of both worlds. This agreement defines the same levels of service provided to the customer as with an MSP agreement, but focused to what is needed to shore up the internal IT staff. For a fixed monthly fee.

a. **Benefits:** The first benefit is one of coverage. You get the benefit of internal knowledge and resource onsite, with the extended resources of the MSP. You still have a much more manageable budget for IT expenses. The

MSP should be available for supporting the internal IT with feedback and suggestions, acting as a sounding board.

b. **Risks:** Not all MSP's are embracing this approach. And some internal IT departments will see the MSP as "the enemy," possibly out to take their jobs. The CoMITs relationship only works if it's a partner relationship with your internal IT, not a vendor relationship.

c. **Why should you do this?:** If you have a good internal IT department that's spending too much time on traditional (i.e., workstation, server support) IT stuff and not enough time specific to your organization (opportunities that generate direct value for your organization). Or you've grown past the capacity of your internal IT resources but don't want to replace them (which could lead to a temporary CoMITs relationship, where the goal of the MSP is to make themselves obsolete over a period of time).

d. **Why shouldn't you do this?:** This cannot be an adversarial relationship. It also can't be a way to hide poor or unmotivated internal IT resources. Your internal IT resources need to be all in and buying into the concept. And your MSP should be set up to do this, not "making a special exception" for you and your organization.

Epilogue: Your Checklist

Okay, you've read the book (you have, haven't you?). Now you need to make a checklist of what your "to do" list is. Here you go:

1. **Determine an IT Strategy.** Internal, MSP, or CoMITs?
2. **What does your current IT look like?** Define your current pieces/parts.
3. **Whining Points.** Does your organization suffer from Whining Points? What are you going to do about them?
4. **Obsolescence.** What in your organization is obsolete? Equipment? Applications? People? What is your risk, and what are you going to do about it?
5. **Backups.** What are you currently backing up? What frequency? Is it tested?
6. **Business Continuity?** Go through the Business Continuity worksheet.
7. **Security.** What's in place for your organization?
   a. **Third Party.** If you don't have the appropriate security expertise, don't pretend. Bring someone in who does.
   b. **Products?** Do you have a set of security products properly configured, maintained, and monitored?
   c. **Process?** Are there processes in place?
   d. **Procedures?** Are there procedures in place?
   e. **People?** Are people trained on security issues? Is the culture in place to take this seriously? Are you taking this seriously?

8. **People.** Are people receiving the proper training (beyond security)? Is innovation rewarded? Do you handle new hires and turnover consistently?

9. **Plumbing.** Do you know how your plumbing works? Enough to know if there are specific bottlenecks?

10. **The Future.** How is your organization going to change over the next two years? How will IT help or hinder your efforts?

I've developed some tools (okay, mostly worksheets) that will help you navigate this process. They're available for free by going to http://Simplex-IT.com/BobsBook. You'll only need to give us your email. We'll also sign you up so you can receive our monthly eNewsletter and invites to our monthly webinars and seminars.

Here at Simplex-IT, we also provide a monthly eNewsletter that contains news and announcements about upcoming events (we try to have at least two webinars a month). Email us at BobsBook@Simplex-IT.com to get on that list. And/or follow us on Twitter at Simplex_IT.

Finally, if you'd like to schedule a time to have a chat with me about these issues (or any other IT and/or organizational issues), email me at BobsBook@Simplex-IT.com. Connect with me on LinkedIn at http://linkedin.com/in/rlcoppedge.

I'd also love to get feedback. Throughout this process, I constantly fought the tendency to get "geekier" for the sake of increasing accuracy. Again, my goal was to help non-technical management understand the parts of IT that they *need* to understand. As an example, I started to write sections about "IPv4 versus IPv6" and "The Basics of DNS" and, of course, "Our

Friend DHCP." In each case, I stopped, pulling back from the precipice of geek cliff diving.

Finally, although I've always wanted to write a book, I have to admit that one of the primary reasons behind this was to generate new business for Simplex-IT, my MSP business. If you're interested in discussing ways we can support your organization, let me know at BobsBook@Simplex-IT.com. I might add that we currently provide support to organizations in Ohio, Florida, South Carolina, Canada, Michigan, Georgia, and Pennsylvania. Yup, we get around.

Okay, this is the part where I summarize, wrap it up, say goodnight, wave bye-bye, and impart visions of the song "So Long, Farewell" from the movie *Sound of Music*. My understanding is that I'm also supposed to leave you with some kind of inspirational message that will fill you with the vim and vigor necessary to really use the contents of this book.

Sorry, but cheerleading isn't my strong point. But I do hope you gained some information that will help you understand, appreciate, and take advantage of Information Technology in your organization—and either improve the existing relationship you have with your current provider of IT support, or help you replace that with a more productive relationship.

69982345R00122

Made in the USA
San Bernardino, CA
23 February 2018